SEVENTEEN SECONDS

'... there is a little part that is always alive. That's the
bomb-fuse ... If anything goes wrong, you'll hear the fuse
run. It's a time clock. You've got anything up to seventeen
seconds. When you hear that fuse run ... jump clean over
ten-foot walls like they weren't there ... you're four
hundred yards away or else.'

The true, heroic story of John Stuart Mould and Hugh Syme,
Australians who volunteered for mine-disposal work in
Britain during World War II, and their many brushes with
death. To them was given the task of dismantling the
deadly acoustic mines ... with seventeen seconds to
blast-off if any false move was made.

SEVENTEEN SECONDS

Ivan Southall

KNIGHT BOOKS
Hodder and Stoughton

ISBN 0 340 20132 0

This is a new and re-written edition of *Softly tread the brave*
originally published by Angus & Robertson in 1960

Text copyright © 1973 Ivan Southall
First published in 1974 by Hodder and Stoughton Ltd,
in association with Hodder and Stoughton (Australia) Pty
This edition first published in 1977
Printed and bound in Great Britain in Knight Books for
Hodder and Stoughton Children's Books, a division of Hodder and
Stoughton Ltd, Arlen House, Salisbury Road, Leicester, by
Cox & Wyman Ltd, London, Reading and Fakenham

Contents

Preface

I have prepared this special edition of 'Softly Tread the Brave' for young people, and that does not mean a gutted edition.

It is written with economy and directness and relates events that upon second reflection, I think young people should know.

It is the story of some of the exploits of two mine disposal officers of the Second World War – both now dead.

It is founded upon diaries, comtemporary notes, tape-recorded statements, interviews and official documents. All characters are, or were, real people. It is not a story of combat, but a tribute, however inadequate, to the gigantic stature of the human spirit. This was self-discipline and courage truly beyond understanding – as ordinary men rendered safe the live weapons powerful enough to level a city block and vapourise their bodies. That these men were not drugged or mad or insensitive, but were normal emotional human beings is a matter of some moment.

Shortly before his death John Stuart Mould dictated an account of his experiences, and to it has been added information from other sources, particularly from the late Hugh Randal Syme. Without Mr Syme's technical guidance and remarkable courtesy over a long period this book would not exist.

In addition, I thank John Hetherington, Mrs Margaret Mould, Mrs Gladstone Heath, Miss Bettye Davidson, David Syme and Company, The Herald-Sun (Melbourne), The Naval Archives Branch of the Department of Navy, The Admiralty, Oxford University Press, and the University Building Bookshop, Melbourne.

CHAPTER 1

The thin men

They were thin men. It was surprising how thin they were. Churchill said they were different from ordinary men; gaunt, said Churchill, and haggard. Their eyes were bright and their faces were blue.

They could be the most patient of men yet the most impatient; the most temperate and the most intemperate; the clearest of mind and the most exhausted. When they slept, they died. When they died, there weren't any bits to pick up. When they died they flashed into eternity in the thousandth part of a second.

The telephone rang, and Mould answered it. 'RMS duty officer here.' Mould liked the sound of that. Today he was somebody for the first time.

'Sir,' said the voice. 'Is that you, sir?'

It was, and Mould drawled again. 'RMS duty officer here. Can I help you?'

'Oh gawd, sir, I've lost him.'

Mould stiffened, his sense of importance suddenly adrift. He had not been somebody long enough to handle hysteria.

'He's gone, sir. I've lost him.'

'Now p-pull yourself together, sailor. Who's gone?'

'Oh gawd. There's nothing left.'

'Now c-come along, sailor. N-nothing left of what?'

'Me officer, sir. He was out in the middle of the field, bending over it, sir, and suddenly it was gone. All of it. Everything. It's not fair. There ain't no God I tell ya.'

For the moment there ain't no God in Germany.

There, caught in the crossed wires of admiration and hatred of Britain, Adolf Hitler has been convinced that bombs do not kill enough people quickly enough. Broken hearts are not broken spirits. A bomb aimed from a high-flying aircraft penetrates the earth like an arrow, and blasts up through the entry hole. The shockwave, beneath the surface, cracks foundations, gaspipes, water-pipes and sewerage, but doesn't maim enough people. There is a weapon that will do this, and Adolf Hitler uses it. It contains more explosive than the heaviest bomb, yet does not penetrate the earth. On a parachute, it drifts to earth, then quietly ticks away seventeen seconds. It cracks. Buildings dissolve into dust. Human beings rip into shreds. It is a terror-weapon, because it cannot be aimed. It lands where it will and kills everybody; soldier, child, saint, and sinner.

Home Security rang the Admiralty one morning. 'I say, old boy!' (At least, one is told it went that way.) 'Jerry's a cad.'

'Hear, hear!'

'He's dropping magnetic mines on London.'

'Balderdash! No naval officer would tolerate such a thing.'

'You come round here, then, and look at this object strung up in a tree.'

The Admiralty rang HMS *Vernon. Vernon* was the School of Torpedoes and Mines built on solid earth down Portsmouth way. 'It's not cricket,' said Admiralty. 'These beastly Huns are dropping magnetic mines on London.'

'Magnetic mines on London?' snorted *Vernon.* 'Poppycock.'

'Gad, they are, sir. The Army doesn't know what to do with them. They've called in the Navy.'

'The Royal Navy?' spluttered *Vernon.* 'On *land,* sir?'

So they called the section, RMS – Rendering Mines Safe – and it was the only operational unit within the walls of the Admiralty. Their ships were Humber Snipe saloons, their seas were the blasted cities and villages of Britain.

Mould got a grip on himself because he still held that telephone. 'Have you got your c-car out there?'

'Yes, sir.'

'You g-get in it and c-come back here and make a full report in person. Got that?'

'Yes, sir.'

'I'll be waiting.'

Mould hung up, shaking and ill. A flash of light, and a man was gone. 'He was leaning over it, and suddenly it was gone. All of it. Everything . . .'

What was Mould doing in a place like this? He was not a fool or a feeble-minded fanatic; not even dedicated to improving his soul. Life was a gratifying state, and he made the most of it – to the despair of his family. He hated routine and discipline and everything that tied him to convention. He did things his own way, always, as he had done this. A week ago he had scarcely heard of these ghastly weapons. Now he was a mine-disposal officer.

At the beginning, Mould had been one of twenty-four amateur yachtsmen who had whooped across the world in the liner *Strathnaver* from Sydney to the Mersey. In their wake, at different times, the Luftwaffe and the German Navy and the U-boat arm had bombed and shelled and torpedoed. Even the mighty *Empress of Britain*, two hours astern, plunged to the bottom of the Atlantic. But they knew nothing of those things, no matter where or when they happened. *Strathnaver* was a little world, cut off, living within itself, while twenty-four yachtsmen were initiated into the elementary mysteries of the Royal Navy.

'Mould,' said Lieutenant Stephenson patiently, 'you may wear civilian clothes but you are a probationary temporary sub-lieutenant, RNVR, and even you, Heaven help us, may some day be an admiral. A probationary temporary sub-lieutenant never goes downstairs, he goes below.'

'Sir.'

'And *never* upstairs. He goes up top.'

'Sir.'

'And when he goes off watch – for what his watch has

been worth – he goes *below* to his cabin, not to his room.'

'Sir.'

'Very good. Carry on.'

'Yes, sir.'

'Well, don't stand like a stuffed dummy. Carry on, Mould.'

'Oh my gawd, I *am* carrying on, aren't I?'

'Mould . . . when I say, "Carry on", I don't mean carry on, I mean get to hell out of it.'

'Yes, sir.'

'In the Navy when you carry on you knock off. You are at present on watch, a special duty. When I say carry on, I mean carry on with normal routine, whatever that may be, if anything. Understood?'

Red didn't have those worries. Red Kessack was a man of many ports and looked like one. He'd skippered a ferry and sailed the high seas in peculiar ships. His accent was a completely original voice, a union of English, Scottish, Australian, and American.

Why had any of them joined the Navy?

There was Hughie, for instance. The Symes were one of Australia's great families. Surely if any man could have found a safe niche it was Hugh Syme. He looked the gentleman – the tall, thin, reserved type. If Hughie resolved to sit on his dignity he sat on it. Why was *he* in the Navy? He liked mucking about in boats, like the rest of them; clerks or carpenters or company directors, they had that in common.

Syme had a half-share in an eighty-two-footer, *Westwind*; Mould borrowed a ride from friends, but it was the common interest that brought 280 men together. It was why they were journeying to Britain: twenty-four probationary officers over thirty years of age and 250-odd ratings under thirty years of age – age was the only reason why one was an officer and another was not. No one man knew more about the Royal Navy than any other, except that the Royal

Navy was accepting recruits and the Royal Australian Navy wasn't.

'Red,' Mould said, 'if the Royal Navy will commission a man with a Board of Trade Yachtsman's Certificate, they can commission me.'

'How long have you had your ticket, Mouldy?'

'I studied for it, boy, specially for the occasion.'

He was a rare bird, this Mould, long and lanky, sandy-haired and blue-eyed, the life and soul of the party. He always looked three parts tight. His was an extraordinary face, tossed carelessly together rather than sculptured, and the smile in his eyes was all but permanent. 'Maybe some join up for King and Country,' Mould said, 'or to keep out of gaol, or to leave their wives. Maybe some are called to defend the rights of man. Red, I just joined the Navy.'

Dudley Reid was another. The tall, athletic type was Dudley; tall, dark, lantern-jawed, with a long face. Reid knew his own mind and expressed his opinions with forthrightness.

So there were four of them out of twenty-four – Dudley, Hughie, Red, and Mouldy – four straws plucked from a bundle; everyday, ordinary men off the chain, but typed to their backgrounds.

Strathnaver steamed into the Mersey in the early hours of 27th October 1940, and was at once intercepted by a destroyer and turned back to sea.

Liverpool had been mined during the night; it was unsafe until minesweepers swept the channel. Magnetic mines were terrible things. In the minds of men who knew them only by name they were spherical, bobbing objects with horns like the devil. In some mysterious manner the mine was attracted to a passing ship like to a magnet, and blew the bottom out of it. That's what they thought. That men in flimsy little ships should sweep these diabolical instruments was one of the lunacies of human nature.

Ahead of them, Britain burned. They knew that, but could not comprehend it. Mould could have been English if his family had not migrated when he was two. He had even returned to England twenty years later to study for his profession. A good architect was Mould, the highest pass of his year.

Ahead of them was Liverpool, mined. Ahead were foundered ships destroyed in their own harbour. Ahead the little trawlers perilously cleared the channel.

In the afternoon, when *Strathnaver* crept in, the grey city lay veiled by smoke and autumn haze. Perhaps the smoke came from burning homes. That, they didn't know, but they were angry and frightened. They had acted the fool for a long journey across the world. They had volunteered for war, many on the war's first day, but had not bothered to analyse it. They knew that France was beaten and that the Fuehrer strutted wherever in Europe he liked. They knew that Britain stood alone. They knew those things, but could not comprehend them.

The harbour and docks were mined, so *Strathnaver* anchored mid-stream. They had arrived, but could not go ashore.

Darkness came, and they heard the sirens, the undulating wail. It was a terrible sound and never, never would be anything less. Ashore, in the gloom of the city, children cried.

The 280 yachtsmen stood on deck and watched a three-dimensional spectacle staged in the fourth dimension of dismay. They heard the thunder of aircraft-engines and the eruptions of earth and heavens. Spires, buildings, chimney-stacks, oily water, ships, cranes, stabbed like flame out of blackness, and a red city crept up from the earth.

HMS *King Alfred* at Hove was the Officer Training School, Royal Navy Volunteer Reserve. It comprised three establishments – Mowden School, Lancing College, and the original King Alfred, which had been built as a vast amusement-centre. There had been a subtle change in all three.

Here were men from the trawlers and the lower decks, others from the Dominions and the Colonies, even from

America. All, if they did not fail, went forth as officers to their chosen tasks. Almost all wanted little ships. There, for a while, war became an adventure again.

The twenty-four yachtsmen needed their weeks at *King Alfred* to educate them to protocol. The Australians, notoriously poor respecters of persons, had to learn that in the Royal Navy one respected persons. The discipline hit them, because Australian discipline was maintained internally and not worn like a mask. The approach of these two dozen gentlemen to problems was rarely traditional. Any senior officer saluted by them stumbled in his stride. When they wished to speak to him, they spoke to him. When they lodged a complaint, they voiced it aloud. When their uniforms didn't fit, they said so.

They sounded out the prospects and plugged for motor torpedo-boats. Mould had misgivings, but went for them nevertheless. Syme couldn't. He was too old. 'A man of thirty-seven,' they said, 'is too staid for that sort of thing. Dash is needed for MTBs. A man of thirty-seven has done his dash. MTBs shake so much that your poor old bones would break. We'll train you for a desk job.'

'Thanks,' said Syme, and hobbled away.

The news got around that Syme was on the retired list, and many with younger bones came to him at quiet moments. 'If anything goes wrong, Hughie, if I get killed or anything, post this letter to my mum.'

One week-end a couple of mysterious characters – lieutenants, RNVR – drifted through *King Alfred* with hands bandaged to the elbows. Red said, 'Holy cow, what's wrong with you guys?'

The mysterious characters conferred in whispers, then announced 'Dermatitis.'

'*Dermatitis?*'

'That's right. Top secret.'

'What's top secret about dermatitis?'

'It's *how* we got it.'

'Does it hurt?' said Red.

'Frightful.'

'Yeah,' said Red, 'but is *this* a hospital?'

'Been to hospital,' they said. 'We're here for new appointments. Got to change jobs. We're allergic to high explosive.'

' 'Struth,' said Red. 'Who isn't?'

'It's this way,' one of them said, 'we're from the Admiralty. We had to delouse German mines. Very painful.'

'You're telling me,' said Red.

The four straws from the bundle had been there three weeks. What they didn't know about the Royal Navy was almost everything. They had heard of Nelson and Trafalgar and *England expects*. They knew a Wren from a magpie; they had guessed it before anyway. They had only the vaguest conception of what was required of an officer, but were prepared to learn if the Royal Navy insisted.

'This is the picture,' the commander said one afternoon. 'I have a signal from Captain Currey. South African fellow. Interesting. Top-secret team he runs up in London. He's looking for volunteers . . . Can't tell you much about the work; the captain will do that, anyway. But you'll be messing about with mines. He wants officers of outstanding courage, enterprise and initiative for special duties ashore and he's heard of our twenty-four Australians who are alleged to be silly enough for anything.'

Mould hooted with laughter, an unforgivable sound in the sacred silence of the quarter-deck. Twenty-three more Australians hooted also, then discerned the atmospheric chill.

'I will leave it to you, Syme,' the commander said coolly, 'as class regulating officer, to record the names of volunteers. It is an honour in the Royal Navy to volunteer. Special duties are the high-road to glory.'

By the time Syme was through he had twenty-one names on the list, and – to hell with desk jobs – added his own to the bottom. Two refused. 'If we'd wanted a job on land, we'd have joined the army.'

In the morning the commander said, 'Gentlemen, the Australian volunteers are Kessack, Mould, Reid and Syme. Congratulations, gentlemen. You are appointed to RMS, Admiralty, under the command of Captain Currey, and will proceed at once to HMS *Vernon* at Portsmouth for training.'

'Excuse me, sir,' said Mould.

'Yes, Mould?'

'RMS. What does it mean?'

'Rendering Mines Safe.'

Later, several heroes with young bones returned to Syme's cabin at odd moments. 'I say, old boy, that letter to my mother. Do you mind if I take it back?'

CHAPTER 2
Take a mine

They went out as self-conscious sub-lieutenants, ignorant of the background and knowledge of procedures demanded of officers. Twenty-three days in a training school could not make a seaman or an officer and didn't.

They stumbled into the maze that was the Royal Navy, surrounded by ranks and departments of which they knew nothing. They couldn't even speak the language, that fence of incomprehensible idiom erected by the Lords and their lieges to baffle lesser minds.

They came to Portsmouth. It was sacred ground; their tread was uneasy. They expected to be stifled by blankets of arrogance and that unique lack of manners they had found some English believed to be graciousness.

They came prepared for a long and intricate course, knowing nothing of mines or high explosives, or, with the exception of Syme, of magnetism and electricity. Surely they would be briefed to the full. Surely, although bad officers, they would not be sent out as bad craftsmen. Getting used to the idea was the problem. There were emotions like wonderment and respect for themselves, and dreadful moments of panic when they wanted to run.

Vernon, they soon learnt, was a top-secret, top-priority, backroom organisation that didn't overpower them. Their expected sense of inferiority was left without a prop. They trod on a dozen corns, but no one trod back.

Vernon was the brains behind the battle of the mines, the laboratory in which enemy weapons were defeated and new weapons were devised. There were more heroes to the line than in the epics of ancient Greece. But the heroes existed in a slightly unreal world, fighting a war that was never less than a challenge to their intelligence and was at times oddly abstract.

'How long will you be here, gentlemen? A couple of days perhaps. Pulling these things to bits is elementary!'

They were in the commander's cabin . . .

'You would be right to call it a war of nerves, but you're not fighting God or the devil. What man has put together, you can take apart. It depends upon the attitude of mind.

'You have the privilege of saving thousands of lives, a privilege not given to many. You save those lives directly and indirectly by rendering weapons safe that represent an immediate threat and a remote one.

'All the mines you will face for the time being will fall upon land. It is upon the sea that the enemy wants to cripple us, but he must master all elements if he is to invade this island. He is dropping mines on land because mine-laying aircraft cannot lie idle while bomb-carrying aircraft work.

'At sea, mine-warfare is an endless and fluctuating battle. He introduces a new mechanism, and we have to crack it. If we don't, the minesweepers cannot sweep – and so ports are closed and this island starves.

'You may be asked to render safe a weapon no one has seen before. Until you defeat it on land our scientists cannot defeat it at sea. Hence we have Ouvry and Lewis and Baldwin at Shoeburyness last November cracking the first magnetic mine when the war was only two months old. The Hun thought we wouldn't crack it for two years. These are the issues that win or lose wars.

'*Vernon*'s task is to keep the sea-lanes open, but we are asked also to reopen the cities. Unexploded mines can close up cities just as sea-lanes can be closed.

'You may ask how does mere man stand up to this kind of strain? Some are devout and some are profane. Some get drunk and drown their fears. One mentality demands an understanding of the mine that he may know exactly what produces a given effect, and, armed with that knowledge, he will render the weapon safe with confidence. Another mentality may prefer to know how to do the job, but not why he does it. Neither man is strictly right or strictly wrong while he is concerned only with rendering a weapon safe.

'To a large degree you will not be subject to tiresome regulations. You will obey our orders, but you are the *élite*. As such, others will regard you; for that you have the assurance of Winston Churchill. For you, gentlemen, nothing is too good. Whatever you command will be done. When you come to a mine, no matter where it lies, *everyone* will do as you ask.' He coughed. 'We have noticed that respect from others induces in us humanity rather than arrogance.'

They were in the mining-shed ... 'This is the magnetic mine.

'How does it strike the ship? Hell, it couldn't if it tried. No, sir, this doesn't go chasing ships. This one sinks and sits and meditates.

'It's got a magnetic set-up in it – this contraption in the cradle – about the size of a tea-caddy. All ships are magnetic. They pick it up from the earth's field while they're being built; red polarity in the northern hemisphere, blue in the south. The beating of the hammers, the lie of the land, electrical storms. All sorts of things bring it about. And everything that goes into the ship; the wiring, the engines, the cables, the hawsers. Every fragment of ferrous metal is loaded with magnetism. So when a ship comes near a magnetic mine the needle in the unit moves. If the pull is strong enough, it closes an electrical circuit and fires the detonator; then the detonator fires the primer and the primer fires the main charge. Up goes three-quarters of a ton or more of improved TNT and cracks the bottom of the ship like a cold dish on a hot stove. Ships go down so fast that crews are left standing. Of course, to counter it we degauss our ships – *change* the magnetism – but you chaps will not be worrying about that.

'So, if you want to live, remember that every fragment of

20

ferrous metal is magnetic. Before you go near one of these little beauties, empty your pockets. Don't wear buckles or tie-pins or suspenders. Hold your pants up with elastic or let 'em fall. Maybe your watch will kill you. Pocket-knives, nail-files, old screws, too. Take anything magnetically alive into its proximity and you'll actuate the unit just as a ship does. But don't let it scare you.

'On land, one part is always alive. The bomb-fuse. Don't let that scare you either. If anything goes wrong you'll hear the fuse run. It's a time-clock. You've got seventeen seconds. So, when you hear that fuse run, you go like hell. You leave racehorses for dead. You jump clean over ten-foot walls. When she goes up you're four hundred yards away or else . . .

'Maybe four hundred yards is a lot of distance for seventeen seconds, but when those glands start pumping you jump clean out of your own way. Of course, it's not so good if the fuse has already run some time. You never know about that. You're up against it if it's only got ten seconds to run, or five seconds, or none. In that case you drop dead.

'You can see the mining-shed. We're still cleaning up after a little charge of TNT – a couple of pounds – that Jerry poked under the rear door of a mine and wired to the bolts. The boys had rendered it safe. It was just routine, taking the rest to pieces. They spun off the nuts, got a hold on the door, and gave it a pull. Punched half the roof off and killed six men. Maybe Jerry thought the mine would go up, but it didn't. Wouldn't have been much left of *Vernon* if it had. These little beauties will level a city block.'

They were on the road. Red sprinted like a maniac until Mould yelled 'Stop!'

They paced off the distance. Red had not run far in seventeen seconds. Hughie said, 'Lord, we're a bit uphill, aren't we?'

They were in the lecture-room taking notes.

They were told how to recognize each type of mine, how to distinguish a particular mechanism and to calculate the area of danger. That way lives and property were spared.

'Of course, gentlemen, there is always the unexpected.'

They were told of tools that had been perfected to make the task safer and quicker for skilled hands.

'All you lack, gentlemen, is experience.'

They were told how to take a live mine to pieces, where to start and where to end.

'Follow that sequence, gentlemen, and you will be safe. Usually, anyway.'

They were told how to burn through the casing of a live mine when the fuse was inaccessible, and thus burn the main charge.

'Sometimes, gentlemen, the main charge will almost burn away before the mine explodes, relatively harmlessly. Sometimes it explodes much sooner.'

They were told how to lower a charge beside a live mine under water in a dock or a canal, to wreck the mechanism without detonating the mine.

'That should work, gentlemen, but sometimes it doesn't.'

They were told where to look for booby-traps and what to do with them.

'We're still learning, gentlemen. It's not the booby trap we know that gets us. It's the one we don't know.'

They were told of new types of mines, and of expected developments and dangers.

'The acoustic unit, gentlemen, is already with us. The first turned up on 6th September when it sank a wooden ship off Inchkeith Light. We have never rendered one safe. If you find what you suspect to be an acoustic mine, send for the experts. Remember, gentlemen, you have much to learn. So have we.'

They took their notes and read them afterwards.

'Seems to me,' said Red, 'there's one thing we've learnt for sure.'

Then they were on their way to London.

CHAPTER 3
Room with three doors – London

All night long, German aircraft came and went and a battery of guns blasted into Mould's weariness. One bomb landed close enough to shake the bed and shatter his nerves.

He had to report to the Admiralty at nine, and he emerged from his hotel red-eyed and disconcerted, with the eclipse of his inherent good humour leaving him empty. Half Moon Street was deserted. He had imagined that debris was at once attacked by an army of men with shovels and wheelbarrows and three-ton trucks. Bomb-debris, he had imagined, would be a scene of human activity, a living assertion of the British spirit. He had not expected to see it like this, passively accepted.

He climbed the rubble, damaging his shoes and soiling his clothes, and stamped down into Piccadilly. The road was wet. Here and there were a taxi, a bus, a bicycle, a few citizens on foot dressed in black. The sky was grey with mist and cloud and smoke and drifting barrage balloons.

'Good morning. Going my way?'

A taxi was there, and a naval officer was greeting him from it.

'I'm going to the Admiralty,' Mould said.

The door swung open, and Mould clambered in.

'Haven't seen you around.'

'No,' said Mould, puzzled, because the face seemed familiar.

'Australian?'

'Yes.'

'Joining RMS?'

'That's just what I'm doing.'

'It's a small world. I'm Greville McClinton.'

'I'm Mould ... And *you* had dermatitis! You were at *King Alfred*!'

McClinton grinned. He showed his hands. 'Clean as a whistle again, but I'm going back to sea. What's your trouble, Mould? You look miserable.'

'You know what it's like. First time you make a speech or dive from a high board.'

The corridors of the Admiralty went this way and that, on and on.

'It's not a bad show,' McClinton said. 'Drive round in top brass saloons. Army chauffeurs. Everyone worships you. But you see some terrible things. The Old Man's just waiting to get his hands on you chaps. Real empire-builder, the Old Man.'

It was a narrow room with three doors – the door through which they stepped and two more, one at either end. There were tables and a chair or two, a bomb-fuse here and there, charts on the walls, and stillness. It felt cold, like a cave chipped out of rock.

'Where's everybody?' said Mould.

'In bed or the Midlands. Up there they've been belted lately. The ports have been getting it, too. We're short-handed. That's why you chaps are in. That's the Old Man's door. That's the ratings' mess at the other end. You'll be allotted a rating and a driver later.'

'I thought we were on our own?'

'We are. The ratings back out of harm's way before we start.' McClinton chuckled. 'Ratings are not allowed to get killed.'

'Why should they be killed if it's not necessary?'

'They shouldn't, Mould. They certainly should not ...'

Syme arrived hours late, anxious and agitated. Mould and Red and Reid were obviously installed well ahead of him. The officer of the day, Miller, peered from behind a desk. 'You're Syme?'

'That's right, sir.'

'You've been adrift, old boy.'

'Yes.'

'When you're ordered to report at 0900, Syme, that's what it means.'

'I know. I'm sorry.'

'The Captain's waiting for you. I suggest you don't waste time.'

It was a bad start, and there was nothing in the Old Man's cabin but the Old Man himself.

'Well, Syme, so you're with us.'

'I'm sorry, sir . . . I'm not accustomed to Service life. It's my fault entirely.'

'Sit down, Syme.'

Hughie sighed into a chair.

'Tell me about yourself, Syme.'

'I'm thirty-seven, sir. A clerk.'

'A clerk?'

'That's what my father used to say.'

'But what did you say?'

'I was with *The Age* newspaper in Melbourne. I did science and civil engineering and industrial management, and fooled about a lot.'

'What was your job – precisely?'

'Works-manager.'

'So how does that make you feel about this?'

'I don't feel much at all, sir.'

'There's an element of risk. You realise that?'

'Yes, sir.'

'I must acquaint you with the facts, Syme. We've lost good men, and you know the maxim: dead men tell no tales. So we don't know *why* we lost them. I can't have any man coming in here with his eyes closed. If you're in doubt, pull out.'

'I won't pull out, sir.'

Currey grunted. 'I'd like to know your reasons.'

That was the question Syme didn't want. Perhaps it was family. 'I don't like the idea of being maimed or messed up,

25

sir. I'm told that in this business the end is sharp – and clean.'
Currey kept his thoughts to himself.

No two men came at it from the same point of view, though Mould, like Syme, was terribly unsure. Red was unduly boisterous, but in unguarded moments his face was long-drawn. Dudley Reid was there by concession only. He had felt duty-bound to volunteer, but he intended to go to sea at the first opportunity; he would remain only until he had done a fair share.

They met the ratings and drivers who were to work with them. As sub-lieutenants they were to be driven in the style of admirals and Cabinet Ministers, but junior officers in chauffeur-driven saloons were not objects of envy. In their first day they sensed that they were alone. The courage to be demanded of them was *different*. Emotion and passion and hatred would only kill them. Never could they respond to a battle-call or to the conviction that an enemy must be driven back because he was wrong and they were right. Never could they step out of themselves in anger or in pride. Calmness and steadiness in the face of crippling human fears; these were the qualities they would have to find. Could a man, constantly confronting these things, remain unbroken? This squad was so small, fifteen in all, new recruits included. The experienced men worked night and day at the limits of endurance.

The new men were asked to learn quickly. Soon the experienced officers would be too worn to carry on. That was why McClinton was there – recalled to pass his knowledge on. And others helped; Miller and Giddon, Fortt, Riley, Fenwick and Newgass as they passed through from one part of England to another. From one they would catch a glimpse of something, and would seek clarification from another.

They were in school again.

'These mines sometimes fail to explode on impact because they're not true bombs. No impact-fuse like a bomb. It's the self-destruction fuse, the fuse designed to protect them from sticky-fingered people like us, that fires them on land. Fires them in shallow water just the same, any water less than twelve feet deep. Even then, if they hit hard, the works can be damaged and may not fire. That's why they come down on parachutes. There's an inertia weight that slides in a groove at impact, slides quietly and releases a spring-loaded pin to start off the cycle that ends with the explosion. But the weight can stick, just as the clock can stick after it's run a second or two. A fragment of grit in there, or dust. That's why you do *not* move the mine. One more jolt may dislodge the weight or release the clock, before you have given a thought to things like magnetism.'

They saw that in the genius of man his thoroughness could be his defeat. 'This mechanism is beautifully done – like a swiss watch. But he has made a mistake – and saved thousands of British lives in the making of it. The mistake is why we're able to render it safe. The mine is far deadlier than the bomb, and if he learns of this mistake the mine may be unbeatable on land. So that's a warning, gentlemen. Idle tongues cost lives. This information is survival or death. He hardened the inertia weight – as simple as that. Had he left it unhardened it might never have bounced, might never have stuck in the groove.

'Perhaps you begin to see which mines are the nasty ones. Anything standing on its nose for any reason is very, very dangerous. A knock can free the weight and fire the fuse, so easily, unless the clock has jammed. And that could have happened anywhere between one second expired and firing-point. It could have run its full course and jammed an instant short of firing. You're not to know. Any mine not decently flat is a very nasty customer. If it's tail-down, at least the weight can't fall, but you still have everything else; clock, primer, detonator, and magnetic unit.

'Always plan your escape. You might be in a warehouse on the Thames, four or five floors above the river. You appreciate that in seventeen seconds you can't get down many stairs. It's better to leap through a window or a loading-door into the mud below, no matter how far below, and take your chance.

'Blast does odd things, so prepare for the unexpected. If you're in a field, head for a haystack. A haystack's first class. Or get behind a hedge or in a ditch. Don't change your mind half-way. Get where you're going.

'If you're down a sewer or up a lamp-post, have a rope or a ladder handy. You can't expect a friend to wind on a windlass. If you don't know how to use a rope, learn. If you're slow on a ladder, speed up.

'Then there are times when there isn't an escape route. You never know when you'll have to spring like the devil. Keep fit. Some of the boys take a run in the park every morning.'

Syme lay awake for nights, rehearsing in his mind the step-by-step procedures, forcing into his mind pictures of the mechanism, determined to understand the nature of every component, its causes and effects. He had not told them he was deaf in his right ear. Until he strained to hear the whir of a running fuse he had not imagined it would be important.

Mould, too, lay awake, concerned not so much by *why* a thing worked, but *how* it worked. Mould saw it as a whole; Syme saw it in parts. Each mind, ultimately, would produce the same result, but by different methods. Their common ground was fear – the one thing they did not discuss.

But it was a fact that some survived, or this world of theirs would have been peopled only by ghosts. It was a fact that the veterans of the trade were cheerfully fatalistic, but they loved life and wasted none of it.

The hours of apprehension and learning lengthened to a week, and the time came for Mould to be duty-officer. Then the moment came for the telephone to ring and for the sailor to say: 'He was out in the middle of the field bending over it, sir, and suddenly it was gone. All of it. Everything . . .'

CHAPTER 4
The smell – Kent

The telephone again, ringing at six in the morning, and it was dark and cold and felt like the middle of the night. Mould was not asleep. He had not yet learnt how to sleep.

The voice said, 'Is that you, Mouldy?'

'Yes.'

'Duty officer here. How are you? Bright and beaming?'

'Yes.'

'You've got your first job. Pile out and report in half-an-hour.'

He reported in the half-hour, and his brain was numb; he found himself at the Admiralty but couldn't remember how he got there. McClinton walked out. 'Hullo, Mouldy. Ready for the fray?'

Mould followed. 'Are you g-going to help me?'

'It's your mine, Mouldy, but I'll be there.'

Everything flowed in its accustomed routine, McClinton's rating in front with the army driver, the bag of anti-magnetic tools in the boot, and the car purring out of the yard, up the ramp, into deeper darkness.

Mould sat on the edge of the seat, starched, at first thinking of nothing. Before the mind of a man in the near-dead hour a life-time is supposed to flash.

McClinton was talking. 'The mine's down at Sole Street. It's a railway station in the country. Supposed to be quaint . . .'

McClinton was talking, but Mould wasn't listening. It was a voice in another room. Yesterday, with the fuse on the desk, he had done it again and again and again, sure in the end that he could have done it blindfolded and had shut his eyes to prove it. He could remember now the starting point, but beyond that it was an aching blank. The tremble was in

29

his hands, and already he was intensely cold. McClinton would be there to lean on.

The drill! The gag to the top of the bomb-fuse – that extra-ordinary instrument, the gag – screwed to the threaded top of the bomb-fuse. No! First pump it up, because the gag forces air under pressure into the tiny holes in the top of the bomb-fuse to deceive the mine into initiating the sequence it follows in the sea. There the weight of deep water depresses a rubber diaphragm and causes a safety-pin to render the self-destruction fuse harmless. Air pressure does the same thing. Next comes the bronze spanner to shift the threaded ring that locks the bomb-fuse . . .

It was daylight, damp, with low clouds and greyness, and this was Sole Street. They had asked, 'Where's the mine?'

'That way.'

They had gone that way and asked again.

'Down there. There's a policeman.'

The policeman had a round face that peered in at Mould.

'Good morning, sir.'

Everything was dreamlike. Mould's head was light and far above him. What happened on earth was indistinct.

The car moved off and stopped again. McClinton said, 'There's your mine, old chap.'

Outside, the air was bitter, and Mould stuffed his clenched hands into his pockets. He stamped his feet and heard the bag of tools and a bucket clatter out of the boot.

McClinton was opening the gate of a flat field, newly ploughed and wet. The field was the whole world. If any-thing lay beyond it, mist rubbed it out.

The mine looked like the trunk of a chopped-down tree far away.

The car began to reverse down the narrow road.

'Where's he going?'

'Out of danger. Cars are valuable.'

Mould nodded glumly.

They waddled in, squelching, slipping, kicking their

ankles. Their paces became slower and deliberate, and the note of the car engine passed beyond hearing. Now the mine looked like a large concrete pipe pushed at an angle into the ground; beside it was a blur of colour and a tangle of ropes.

'A hundred and fifty yards,' McClinton said. 'Near enough.'

Mould didn't speak.

'We'll have the shovels,' McClinton said to the rating. 'That's your first step, Mouldy. Where there's not a ditch or a hedge or a haystack, dig a hole, and when you've dug it remember *where* you've dug it.'

They dug deep enough and wide enough for two men to get their heads below ground level. The physical labour warmed Mould. He made a mental note of it. Physical labour – beneath the dignity of officers, but helpful.

Now the rating trudged towards the road.

'Right,' said McClinton. 'I'm for the hole and you're for the mine.'

'Alone?'

'You didn't imagine I'd be doing it?'

'No.'

'If the bomb-fuse starts running, you start running, back to this hole.'

'A hundred and fifty yards in *this* kind of mud?'

'It's a very fair distance. It's not my mine and not my risk.'

Mould couldn't hear a bird or an animal or a breeze – nothing but McClinton.

'I understand,' he said. 'It's jolly d-decent of you to be here at all.'

He went through his pockets, then took the tools and the bucket which was now filled with water.

'Mouldy . . . Identify it before you tackle it. And if you're in trouble come back. Don't shout. And don't talk to yourself while you're at it.'

'Yes.'

'Good luck.'

There lay the long grey cylinder askew in the ground, six feet high. The rest was buried. The brute gleamed in what light there was, and the green blur was the parachute, and the ropes were the woven rayon cords of the parachute, and Mould was on his toes treading like a thief. Fuse and detonator were accessible. Yes, they were. Eighteen inches above ground-level. Fear and fright almost crippled him.

McClinton was there; but only his head.

The one life in danger was Mould's. Better by far, surely, to explode this thing from a distance. There was nothing to be flattened by blast. There'd be nothing but a hole in the ground. Why do it at all?

It was magnetic, type C; serial numbers stencilled on the casing. And there was a smell, new to Mould, distinctive and strong and difficult to define. Not the mud, not the parachute; *it was the mine*. Would a man ever forget it? If ever he left this field!

McClinton was watching.

Mould put his tools down in order of use on a piece of hessian. Terrified. God; would he remember the drill? Would it *really* matter if he said *no*?

The gag had to be prepared, that incredibly primitive old-fashioned motor-horn clipped to a straight length of brass tubing. There was a tap in the tube, and a threaded end to the tube. To the thread Mould connected a bicycle pump, opened the tap, and started pumping until the bulb was hard to the touch. All the time he trembled, and McClinton watched, and the mine waited.

He tested the bulb for leaks, placing it in the bucket of water. A leak could kill him. Dwindling air-pressure in the bomb-fuse would allow the safety pin to rise so that the first turn of the spanner would start the clockwork.

No bubbles.

Mould closed the tap and unscrewed his pump, then knelt in the mud beside the mine, miserable with terror. Somehow he had to stop trembling, or he would dislodge the weight or shake the clockwork free by fumbling. Perhaps

32

that had happened two days ago to the man in the open field. Had he fumbled, and fired one ton of high explosive?

This horrible gag. So awkward and clumsy. So much fiddling with it, screwing on the adaptor made to fit the bomb-fuse, screwing it to the mine itself, feeling for the touch of it, listening to the sound of it, and *waiting* for God knows what.

McClinton's head had gone.

Turning that gag on, praying for threads to mate. Fumbling and stiffening and waiting and listening. Wet knees and awful discomfort and uncontrollable trembling. Resting and turning a bit more and listening for buzzing noises and shaking the silence. Tightly home. Tightly. So he put his ear to the fuse and turned the tap and instantly it clicked. Air-pressure popped that safety pin home.

Sweat poured from Mould; sweat and whimpering sounds.

The heavy pin-spanner, that was next, designed to remove the ring that locked the fuse into the mine. All thumbs was Mould, and the gag obstructed him. It felt as big as a house, and somehow around its edges he had to use the spanner while the inflated bulb pressed against his arm and nagged at his nerves. Perhaps even now air-pressure was leaking. Perhaps this. Perhaps that. Perhaps everything was stuck an instant short of impact.

The keeper-ring was turning away, scraping faintly in the body of the mine, and it was lunacy. If he had to run he'd be too weak to move. Then his shaking hands were taking the keeper-ring away from the bomb-fuse, along the length of the brass tube, like a bangle along a skinny arm. Shaking hands that he commanded to be still.

Mould steadied, and drew from the mine a silvery shining cylinder on the end of the dangling gag. The bomb-fuse. Small enough to cup in his hand. Screwed into its business end was a small black tube, the gaine, packed with enough high explosive to fire the mine; enough, even now, to kill Mould if he fumbled.

It took five full revolutions to unscrew the gaine, to bring the horrid thing into his right hand. He shook out the explosive, a solid lump, but still held the bomb-fuse with its tiny detonator inside it; tiny, but destructive enough to blow off his arm. In the side of the fuse were two screws, opposite each other, one leading to the spring-loaded striker, the other to the anvil. Between them sat the detonator; all this hanging on the end of the gag. Mould scratching away at waterproofing compound to get at the smaller screw, then threading out a tiny solid cylinder, the anvil, as bright as new silver. He turned the fuse on edge as he had been shown how to do, averted his face, and allowed the detonator to fall so light in his palm he scarcely knew it was there, and his heart-beat was thundering all over his body. All that agony for only the beginning! Nothing was out but the self-destruction fuse. Everything else was still to go.

The screwdriver again, this time to the plate over the main detonator, which lay dead centre in the looming body of the mine, wedded in there to the spring-loaded primer, waiting only for an electrical impulse to blast Mould to eternity. Four screws, so patiently, so carefully, so silently threaded from the casing, and the plate, about four and a half inches in diameter, lifted gently away. It was inhuman. It was madness. The big black bakelite bung, there it was inside, and the detonator deeper yet.

The bung spanner, that grotesque bronze-handled weapon that could have brained a man; its four tongues guided painfully into the four slots of the bung, and Mould, against the roaring protest of his blood, took the strain. The bung squealed, and every hair on his head prickled.

He waited, listening, cursing silently.

He took the strain again. Suddenly the bung was moving, turning quietly, loosely enough to spin out. There it was, the detonator, the bakelite back of it and its vital terminals, one black, one red. Two thin wires running through the body of the mine to the tail, up there. Inside the tail the same wires passing through a nine-volt battery to the magnetic unit.

That was where oblivion could come from. Mould cut the wires, and the known danger was over. Now only the unknown could kill – the odd chance, the freak, the booby-trap. If a booby-trap did lie in there unseen, he wouldn't know. The man to find it was not the man to see it.

It was a long-headed block spanner now, feeling for two slots in the detonator itself, and Mould was turning until it came loose, and out, dangling on the cut wires, harmless now, a pencil-thin copper tube not two inches long threaded into a bakelite base.

Back to the primer-casing beneath the cavity from which he had drawn the self-destruction fuse. Again the wearying, trembling routine with a ring-spanner that felt as heavy as lead. Turn after turn, until the keeper ring came away violently. The primer plug slammed at him, shockingly, twanging on the end of a powerful spring two feet long.

He was almost sick with the fright of it. He had *forgotten*. Would he ever forget it again! So he fished for the primer, deep in the body of the mine, with a rod of phosphor-bronze, a rod with two spring-loaded claws and a centring plug of wood. The claws clicked home, and Mould got his primer out. Harmless-looking object, like a cocoa-tin or an ignition coil, packed with enough picric-acid pellets to blow the roof off a house. He scratched the solder from the cap and wrenched it off with a twist of his wrist and emptied the pellets over the explosive shaken from the gaine. He set a match to them, and they burnt with a foul, dense smoke.

He was exhausted, but there was still the hydrostatic clock, the device that triggered the magnetic unit under water. Harmless on land *unless* the Germans had packed an explosive charge behind it. Mould would never know until he pulled death into his face. Another spanner and another keeper ring, another crisis of nerve and decision, another agony. The clock was in his hands. He wrested it out with his eyes shut – and cut the wires, all six of them.

'I've done it.'

He was alive.

'I've done it.'

Everything was there on the hessian beside him: bomb-fuse, gaine, detonator, primer, hydrostatic clock. And he was alive.

'I've done it.'

Somebody was shaking him by the hand. Was it McClinton?

'Well done . . .'

CHAPTER 5
The silence – Birmingham

Everything started with the telephone. Syme groped for it, and when he hung up his understanding was vague. Something about a blitz on Birmingham. 'Pile out, Hughie. Grab yourself a change of clothes. There'll be a car along in half an hour.'

Would you believe it! Two fifty-five a.m., 12th December 1940.

He stared into the depths of his cold room, acutely depressed, yearning to lie down again, yearning for the warmth of the bed and its security. Three o'clock in the morning!

He shaved and dressed and packed resentfully, and the things he couldn't take he locked in a suitcase, and the suitcase he locked in the wardrobe. How long would he be away? They'd robbed him once already. Nice people. He locked the room and pocketed the key, still depressed, even angry.

Two days ago Half Moon Street had been mantled with snow, beautiful enough to stir him, until he had gone up to his room and found it ransacked. Yesterday the snow in Half Moon Street had been a filthy yellow slush. Now at 3.30 a.m. it was frozen in ruts and ridges.

He trod carefully to Piccadilly, cold striking at him, cold cutting through him. In a year or two he would be forty, but this was fear as he had never known it. In Birmingham, somewhere, in a street, a park, a canal; somewhere in Birmingham his first magnetic mine!

There was the car, its washed-out lights nosing along the kerb. 'That you, Hughie?' Sounded like Gilbert Stubbs; that at least was something. Gilbert was a good pal. 'Cold this morning, Hughie. Brrr. Hop in. Quick about it. How do you feel? Beetles and butterflies?'

'That's about it.'

Gilbert guffawed, as he had a habit of doing. 'I'm looking after you *and* looking forward to it. Nasty frost, Hughie. Roads are bad. Stuff that suitcase out of the way. Here, take some rug. Seen Birmingham before?'

'Never.'

'Cold up there too. Black frost this morning. Very dangerous. Good driver, my chap. Birmingham's getting a hammering. Unexploded mines all over the place. Seven cars all on the way to Birmingham. Hungry?'

'Not particularly.'

'Time for that. We're stopping off at St Albans for breakfast.'

Gilbert chattered on and Syme thanked God for him.

The St Albans rendezvous was the White Hart. Eight officers and fourteen men were expected at seven o'clock. They started straggling in an hour early, and some still straggled in an hour late. The unanimous opinion was that they would be lucky to get to Birmingham without mishap. Roads were ice-sheets.

The details of that morning failed to register firmly with Syme. Fragments lived; most was lost. He sensed that Red and Mouldy were confident. The mines they could claim as their own had done strange things to them. Their brittleness had gone. Only Syme was untried. Mould and Red and Dudley Reid had made the grade, but Syme had not made the grade, and there was no guarantee that he would.

Others were there that morning. Lieutenant Miller, officer-in-charge of the party, said to Stubbs and Syme, 'I'm setting up in the town hall. It's the worst raid they've had . . . If the town hall's not there ask a policeman.'

The big car turned north into a grey light in which solids were vague masses. Now they had thrown London off they rushed, sometimes at seventy miles an hour, behind blaring horns which gave them right of passage. Even Gilbert had nothing to say. He sat rigidly while his driver fought the monstrous road. To Syme it was without logic, but these were the orders – crawl through London and rush to Birmingham. That a black frost might have glazed the roads, that cars might be wrecked or lives endangered was never reckoned with. The drive to Birmingham was stagecraft, expected of them for the reason that they were who they were.

Coventry lay ahead, but they diverted and did not sight it. Around it a curtain was drawn. Others had gone in through the curtain to render mines safe, and had been glad to leave. Syme didn't know it then, but the lesson of Coventry was why they rushed to Birmingham. There were times when men needed to know they were not alone. They needed an immediate demonstration of brotherhood on the ruins of their doorsteps. They needed more than that, but they needed that at the start. And so the handful of men arrived in Birmingham, shaken and exhausted. Six cars had been damaged. The seventh came in without a mark; in it was Syme, stunned by the shambles.

The driver was lost, confronted by barricades and rubble and crumbling walls. There were miles of fire-hoses; the huge city steamed and smoked and burned, and its people were pale and silent and watching.

'Is the town hall still standing?'

'Don't know.'

'How do we get to it?'

'Don't know.'

At last Stubbs found a policeman. Under his direction the car moved through bleak back streets. Syme wasn't sure what he felt, but his own mine was at his heart. It was too much to expect that he should weep for the city.

They walked into the town hall, and this was a different kind of damage. Bandaged people, bloodstained, maimed, living and dying. Stretchers and doctors and drab penetrating cold. An uneasy emotion nagged at Syme. Children and young girls. Old men and babies. Blood . . .

Lieutenant Miller had established himself in a remote corner, and there were voices, there were words, as Syme moved through.

39

'They delouse the mines.'

'The bomb heroes.'

It didn't sound real.

Miller had coffee for them. Syme found those minutes un-earthly; the cold, the congestion, the hundreds of voices, the crying babies, Miller's modest corner, the Birmingham map tagged in dozens of places where mines lay, the wardens, the regional officer – that local man who could get any-thing – the terrifying efficiency in which Syme was the one weak link.

'Take this one,' Miller said, and indicated a tag on the map. 'It's outside a local town hall. You'll go along, Gilbert?'

They followed a warden back through that mass of people, into the city again, down to the car. After a while, in the grey morning, Syme saw a policeman at a barricade. Stubbs was saying, 'Righto, Hughie, this is it.'

Shivering in the cold again. Road and footpaths were glazed with ice. There were greetings he didn't hear, move-ments of which he was barely conscious, the rating strug-gling with the tool-bag, the warden pointing, Stubbs discussing the weather.

'The area's cleared over a radius of four hundred yards. Not a soul in there.'

People were calling, 'God bless you. Good luck.'

Now they walked, Stubbs, Syme and the rating, past silent factories, empty houses, deserted streets a long way in. Damage was not severe. The mine that would have wrecked the district had failed to explode. It was, as Miller had said, outside a town hall and superbly on its own, parachute lines tangled in telephone wires (all that magnetism) and the mine itself driven two feet deep into the pavement, leaning off the vertical at a dangerous angle. Thirty yards from the mine, round a corner, was a dug-out shelter, and across the road a park.

'Thanks, sailor,' said Stubbs, 'leave everything with us . . . Hughie, you're not to do this by hand. It's a hard one. Use pulleys and cords.'

'Why?'

'The Old Man doesn't want unnecessary risks. It could be booby-trapped. And that angle's bad. You've got a dug-out round the corner so run your cord to it and pull from there. Are you all right?'

'I think so.'

'If you're not, come to me. I'll be at the barricade. There's no disgrace; it's not every man's cup of tea . . . Good luck, old boy . . .'

He marched off like a guardsman, never looking back. Syme was alone in a dead city.

Beginning was the problem, arranging the tools and the pulleys, first pulley to a telegraph pole and the second to a shrub, which allowed him to turn the corner. His hands were raw with cold, and metal stuck to them. Thirty-five yards of cord from the mine to the dug-out. Not far. After all, his first gentle tug to unseat the bomb-fuse could fire the mine. Remote control was not *necessarily* safer. He padded the pavement with layers of hessian where the bomb-fuse would fall.

Eleven-thirty in the morning. That's what it was. And the silence was immense and sagging. His tongue was like sandpaper, so he couldn't spit. And he had to move the telephone wires that were fouling the mine, and the parachute lines, then retrace each move made, each nerve-racking moment, to make *certain* nothing was overlooked.

He pumped up the motor-horn, tested it, and threaded it on to the bomb-fuse; an eternity of numbness, of stillness and cold. He turned the tap, and the safety pin popped home. Slowly then he unscrewed the keeper ring, fumbling with cold, terrified because he fumbled, horrified by his clumsiness, but somehow the ring came back along the shaft of the gag, and then he was resting.

Trees in the park. Frozen garden beds. Why was he looking at them?

The cord; a tanned fishing-line; threaded through the loop on the knurled end of the gag, that end screwed over the

41

bomb-fuse, and knotted with a bowline. Walking back to the dug-out, unsteadily, but getting there, and sensing the importance of 'keeping going'. No more pauses; no more thinking. When he tugged the cord gently he felt the fuse come away, *felt* it hit the hessian, and started counting to twenty. Was the fuse motionless or running?

He walked back, flinching, but everything was silent on the hessian. He removed the gaine and anvil and tiny detonator – even slipped the detonator into his wallet. That was to be his *property*. He drove himself on through peaks of nervous tension that somehow did not turn into screaming, until only the hydrostatic clock was left. That haven for booby-traps! That last point of immeasurable danger because it could be the moment of haste. Syme secured the cord again and limped to the dug-out, old and very tired, then he pulled on the cord.

At that moment he went to pieces on the cold, damp floor, groaning and shaking, but unashamed. He was wishing his father had lived for it; he would have liked him to have known.

After a minute or so, Syme went up the steps into the open air. It was 1.30 p.m. Two hours had gone. He turned the corner and stopped, aghast.

Two boys – not a day over eight either of them – were playing with the hydrostatic clock.

He opened his mouth, soundlessly.

'Hullo, mister. What did you pull the string for?'

Words began to come. '*What in hell are you doing . . .?*'

They were startled by the whisper that became a shriek, and something snapped in Syme. He swore at them and they fled. If he could have caught them he would have kicked them; he'd have cracked their heads together. They beat him by yards, and Syme went back to his mine, wanting to weep over it, overcome by anticlimax. He had groaned and panted and fought fear without restraint because he had been the only man in a half-mile square. He had fought his battle and won in private *with two wide-eyed children in the bushes looking on*. An intolerable cruelty. So he walked heavily back to the barricade, carrying the tools and the bucket and the vital parts of the mine, expecting to find only the policeman. But Gilbert came hurrying, shouting, 'Hughie, are you all right?' Behind Gilbert came the rating, running; behind the rating the policeman; behind the policeman more people than Syme could count. His stride faltered and they over-ran him.

'Jolly good show, Hughie. Congratulations.'

'Congratulations, sir. Give me the bag. Put the things down.'

'They tell us it was your first. Congratulations, sir. I don't know where you get the guts.'

His back was slapped and his hand was pumped. Kids were cheering and women were crying. And they moved him along, out through the barrier and along the road and in through the wide-open doors of the pub.

'To Sub-Lieutenant Syme. God bless him!'

The hat went round, and was presented brimming with coins and notes. 'Speech! Speech!'

What was there to say?

'You can't give money to me,' he said lamely. 'I was only doing my job.'

So they filled him up with beer and sent him on his way, and the day was done.

Next afternoon he had a mine in a field. He drove out with Lieutenant Ronnie Fortt, but stopped off to look at Fortt's own mine. Fortt was an actor, an Englishman, who treated his mines like lines in a play.

Fortt's mine was in the courtyard of a home for old men, in a heap of coke and snow, set up, a sitter, the answer to a disposal officer's prayer. Fortt tucked his cane under his arm and stroked his chin. 'Hughie,' he said, and faded. 'Hughie, old boy. It's too easy. You know, this object has my number on it. It's the 13th December, Friday, and my thirteenth mine. Too easy, old boy. I want something that's going to give me a sweat.'

Syme thought about it. 'You want me to do it?'

'Would you, old boy?'

'I don't mind, if you'll do mine.'

'That, old boy, goes without saying . . .'

Syme was left then with his second mine, a sitter. The fuse was frozen solid, so he treated it with salt. Just an idea that salt would lower the freezing temperature and defrost the fuse. It worked – and there was no need to scrape away the ice. Nervousness was there but he didn't hesitate or tremble or fumble. There was nothing to it when a man was master of himself. It was hard only when things were strange or new or something went wrong. And no more of this remote-control business; he wanted to feel with his fingers. Last night Stubbs had said, 'There's no real reason why you shouldn't do it by hand. Not now. Don't let confidence blind you, but you can take the weight of the fuse in your finger-tips, you can *feel* if there's a booby trap behind it. The same with the clock. The same . . .'

Syme had had a feeling, earlier, that he was not alone. He had walked through the old men's home, from floor to floor, calling out, opening doors, peering into washrooms. He had been certain then, and still was, that two inmates were in the building. 'All right,' he had yelled, 'it's your own risk.'

He had the gag on, had the keeper ring moving through its first turn when doubts hit him. In his bones he knew that something was wrong. He backed off and saw the motor-horn drooping like a tired flower! The air pressure had gone! The bomb-fuse was alive!

It wasn't running, no, but had been disturbed; the merest touch might start it off. That nerve-racking drill; he'd have to go through it again with the bomb-fuse in a thoroughly unpredictable state. Either that or blow the thing up and destroy the home and its damn'-fool inmates with it. He bellowed, 'If you don't want to get killed get to blazes out of there.'

He screwed the gag off, and was ready to run. One movement and he would have gone like the wind. No movement. No sound.

He pumped up the horn a second time and tested for bubbles. Definitely no bubbles. He screwed it on as tightly as he dared, opened the tap and heard the safety pin pop. Fine. So it was back to the keeper ring, but in a moment the tautness had gone again from the horn.

Syme's mouth was turning dry and he was conscious of frozen toes and frozen fingertips and an ache in his ears.

A man *had* to be confident in his tools.

Trembling, he turned the gag off and pumped until he couldn't force another ounce of air into it, and quickly mated it to the thread and spun it back on. The fuse was silent and his tongue was swollen and the tremble was in his bones. The pin popped home.

The keeper-ring. He loosened it quickly and turned it out with his fingers, his other hand tightly over the motor-horn to compensate for air pressure with hand pressure. He withdrew the ring along the brass tube and anxiously took the feel of the bomb-fuse. It felt free, and came safely away.

Urgency. The gaine had to be off the bomb-fuse before escaping air pressure allowed the safety pin to rise. It was instant oblivion in his hands and so damned awkward, hanging on to the thing, unscrewing the thing, even throwing it into the courtyard as far as he could throw, with air pressure dribbling away and the detonator inside the fuse potent enough to blow off his arm. He had joined this outfit because the death was total and clean. Yes? He could have lumps hacked off inches at a time. Squatting in the heap of coke with the bulb tucked under his arm, crushing it to hold the pressure up, scratching at the waterproofing over the anvil with his screwdriver, turning it out with reckless haste, turning it out and holding the detonator in his hand.

Oh, man . . . Tension to unwind. Breath to regain.

Then Fortt's mine blew up. Blast cracked over the silence with frightful force. Syme's impulse was to be sick and run.

But he felt useless. What would there be to find? A monstrous hole? And Fortt gone?

Syme finished his mine. There was nothing else to do. This kind of sickness, he supposed, was a hazard of the trade. He burnt the small explosive charges, collected the pieces and the tools, and got away. Two old men showed themselves and waved.

The Humber was coming along the road. It pulled in and Fortt stepped out. 'Beastly thing,' he said. 'Damaged fuse. Wouldn't shift. Had to blow it up.'

Sub-Lieutenant Mould was astonished by his own aptitude. His fingers were nimble and his brain was quick and the mine was an open book. He had the magic touch.

He drove through Birmingham from job to job in comfort and dignity. Men lifted their hats to him, children touched him, and women regarded him with disarming frankness. A jolly fine show all round. The first in Kent had been hard, but that had been emotional. Already he suspected that the rendering safe of mines was a grossly overrated profession.

The cross on his map was Castle Hill Farm, out on the fringes past the urban line, out where the long-standing black frost had changed to pure white glory, a land frozen stiff to its tips.

The farm was like a bleached chess-board, small hedged areas opening one into the other, and stabbed into the centre of a field was a German magnetic mine, set up like a gigantic decapitated toadstool frozen solid.

The rating lowered the tools. 'Doesn't look good, sir.'

'Stick around,' said Mould, 'until I work it out.'

He crunched across the grass and got down to it. Forty hours it had sat there, freezing harder and harder. Fuse and primer and detonator and clock were locked up inside an armour of ice. He couldn't even smell the thing.

The thread of the fuse was fouled with hoar-frost; even the three tiny holes through which the gag had to exert air pressure on the safety pin were heavily encrusted.

'I'll have a screwdriver, sailor.'

Mould gently prised the blade under the ice to clear the thread. It crackled off with a sound so startling that every nerve in his body leapt to it.

'I don't know, sailor. I don't know about this. Maybe you'd better hop it.'

'I'll stay, sir, until you're ready.'

The field was small and the hedges were close. Too close for safety.

Mould got the screwdriver into it again, a minute jab at a time. Every breaking fragment crackled like breaking glass. 'Buzz off, sailor. I'll be all right.' But the sound down here was so odd that he drew his hand away!

'God . . . *Run like hell, sailor. The fuse.*'

Mould fled for the hedge, but couldn't see a gate or a stile, only the sailor scuttling like a terrified rabbit. He took the hedge in his stride, that sailor did, like a cartoon character through a wall, and Mould went after him, horizontally or vertically or over the top or under it he never knew, but he was blasted into the earth and half the county of Warwickshire seemed to thunder on top of him in lumps and clods, in smoke and mist, like a cloudburst.

After a while they sat up and rubbed the muck out of their eyes. Each confronted an animated heap of mud.

'It's gone off, sir.'

'It has.'

Mould's knees were knocking together.

The field had gone. So had the hedge. Everything had gone except a crater twenty or thirty feet deep and fifty yards wide. Soil lay churned in heaps and ridges and valleys into the fields beyond. 'Gawd,' said Mould, 'did I do that?'

Frightful weapons; he had known; but he had not known *this.*

CHAPTER 6
Christmas party – Manchester

'I suggest,' said the duty officer at 5 p.m. on 23rd December 1940, 'that you chaps pack your bags. Manchester was belted last night, and they're tipping it will collect again.'

At 11 p.m. the Australians were in Manchester.

Mould was appalled by the sound and the violence. He stumbled over hoses and bricks and slates and broken glass. Rescue workers, firemen, first-aid parties, wardens, policemen and servicemen worked within a prison of flame and water and crumbling masonry. Ambulances lurched through burning streets; the injured and dead lay in rows on the pavements.

On foot, the Australians stumbled behind a police officer until they came to Regional Headquarters, where Lieutenant Newgass briefed them. He detailed three mines to each man, then sent them to bed. At first light they were out in the shambles and carnage of the city – and it was Christmas Eve.

Again the smell went with Mould – the dirt of centuries stirred up, the smoke, the stink of mud and extinguishing-fluid, spent explosive, disinfectants, blood, bodies, household gas. The smell and the debris swirled against shattered walls by high pressure water. Mould found himself in Salford, Manchester's sister city. Crowded streets, people staring at nothing; his car abreast of a policeman, in the policeman's arms a boy sobbing.

Gangs were clearing rubble on the fringes of people; shovels and hoses, craters and heaps. Women with shopping-baskets were climbing hills of rubbish.

A reserve policeman waited at Mould's barricade to show him the way. The farther he went the less he liked it. Camouflaged structures towered above his head, camouflaged tanks for oil and petroleum. There was Mould's mine, surrounded by petrol.

He forgot the women with baskets clambering over rubble. He forgot the boy sobbing in the policeman's arms.

Syme walked a long straight street of drab and silent terrace houses, bombed houses. In four hundred yards there was not another living creature.

'Down here,' said the policeman.

Another straight street of drab and silent houses.

'There, sir,' said the policeman.

Syme walked on alone to a house with a hole in the roof and a great green parachute wrapped like a scarf about it. Inside, a narrow passage and a door to the parlour. Inside the parlour, against the wall at the window, a mine in unquestioned possession, a giant of a mine as high as the ceiling and thrust eighteen inches deep into the floorboards.

The clock was going. There were books and newspapers and armchairs. Perhaps the woman of the house would appear with a cup of tea. That was how it felt. Then Syme saw the budgerigars, caged in the window, as forlorn as if they knew. So he strode four hundred yards to the barrier with the cage and all the way back again.

The mine had landed the wrong way round. Bomb-fuse and primer were hard against the wall.

Syme could reach them with his fingertips, but could not work on them, even with the new gag, he could not apply even that. This little tool of brass just devised, to depress the safety pin inside the fuse with a blunt needle. Once in place it could not fail. But the fuse was against the wall, beyond reach . . .

Syme sat in an arm-chair, in the silence, and thought about it.

Red Kessack's house also had a hole in the roof. Also had a parachute flowing over. Also was one of a terrace, grey and drab.

Red tiptoed in and looked up. Above his head was pale light from the roof three storeys high, beneath him an unyielding darkness. The mine had crashed through the slates, through three floors, and into a cavity underneath.

Red felt sad for himself. He'd had problems before, but nothing like a mine he couldn't see. So what was beneath the house? A cellar, a sewer, or what? The smell was staleness and dampness and mustiness stirred up. If there were cellars there must be stairs.

Red gave the hole wide clearance – he was worried about the strength of the floor – and made his way round the walls to the back of the house, quietly turned the latch and viewed a succession of tiny, dismal, deserted yards enclosed by eight-feet-high brick walls, looking as cheerless as prison cells. Steps descended to a doorway.

Red went down. He could distinguish nothing inside until he struck a match. A tight passage receded into darkness. Red edged in, anxiously striking matches, until he came to a horrible little cellar, like a dungeon. In there, in the flare of light, he saw his mine, wedged upright by broken timbers. It had missed a camp-bed by one inch. Blankets had been flung against it. The awakened sleeper had left at a high rate of departure, but there was no humour in the situation. Bomb-fuse and primer could not be seen. They were on the other side, totally out of reach.

The match died, and the walls of the cellar felt incredibly close. Red was uneasy that a human being should be required to sleep in this place – and that *he* should be required to render the weapon safe was monstrous. A splintered beam was jammed between mine and wall, denying, to the most skilled fingers, any real hope of access.

Red backed into the doorway and leant in darkness, awfully alone.

How would others see the problem? How would Newgass or Miller or Giddon or Riley tackle it? The more he thought about it the more he was convinced that he would have to encircle the mine with his arms and turn it. It weighed more than a ton, but he would have to turn it vertically in the most dangerous of all positions. Lurch it – and trigger it! He had to take the risk of blowing up the street because in it was the only chance of saving the street.

If the fuse ran, what then?

If the fuse ran, where could he run? Out of this passage and up the steps and into the yard . . .

He walked into the yard and was surrounded by an eight-foot wall. No escape, not even if he scaled the wall, because he would be confronted by another wall. The only escape was back through the house and into the street, passing directly over the mine. Time could not be stretched. Time was too short for him to reach the street.

Already the words were in his mind, the worn-out words he had read a hundred times in a hundred stories. He would die like 'a rat in a trap'.

Hugh Syme considered his problem. The mine against the parlour wall had to be turned or it could not be rendered safe. It was possible that the first movement would detonate it. That risk was unavoidable, yet only by accepting it could anything constructive be done. He must turn it or burn it, but a fire of the magnitude of a burning mine would raze the district. It could not be turned by manpower, but to bring a machine, an internal combustion engine, within reach of the mine would explode the mine. It would have to be turned by remote control.

Impossible?

He considered the tools at his disposal; a few hundred feet of fishing line, a few shackles, a few spanners. Not by any exercise of imagination could that kind of equipment turn a mine.

Then it dawned, faintly, but with exciting and accelerating detail. A cable – from somewhere a non-magnetic cable – secured to the mine and passed through the window. Directly opposite was a telegraph pole, so perfectly placed that it could have been set there by God. At the corner, on his own side, was another telegraph pole providentially placed.

Syme's excitement grew as he paced the distance to the corner – near enough to a hundred yards. That made five hundred to he barrier. He couldn't bring power inside the barrier, so he would operate outside it, on a cable a third of a mile long. One end of the cable he would turn twice about the mine and shackle it to the lifting lug. The cable would then pass through the open window, take a right-angled turn at the post opposite, a second right-angled turn at the corner post, then straight to the barrier. That end he would shackle to the axle of the car.

It was *good*. The cable would need to be light and supple, the forward movement of the car gentle, and the elasticity of the cable should ensure that the mine pivoted on its nose, held upright by the hole in the floor.

A barrage balloon was high overhead, like a kite on a string.

Miles distant, Mould moved on. The mine beside the petrol-tank had come apart easily. It had only *looked* like a heart-breaker. While others faced terrifying difficulties, Mould went from mine to mine with increasing skill – and began to revert to type. His swagger, his noisy good humour, even his vanity, blossomed again. He respected the mine, but knew that his courage was equal to it.

He found himself directed to a shattered railway-yard. Here had been a cattle train. He searched through disintegrated animals. For three-quarters of an hour, in that frightful place, he looked for his mine, but it had gone, and in going had caused the very mess in which he searched.

He escaped into the dead city, into the lanes of the slums, and was confronted by Lieutenant Ronnie Fortt. There was often something splendid about Fortt. Always the actor. Always immaculate.

'Hullo, Ronnie. Where you off to?'

'Round the corner, old chap.'

'Join you?'

'Of course.'

They walked together.

'What's the trouble?' said Fortt.

'No trouble. Just filthy mess.'

'Yes,' said Fortt, 'one does see it, doesn't one?'

They turned the corner, and here was Fortt's mine, a bicycle leaning against it.

'These people,' he said, 'are fools or angels.'

Mould wheeled the bicycle away, left Fortt to his task, and walked on through the silent city. At a barricade he found Red Kessack talking to a policeman.

'Mouldy, are you busy?'

'Not notably.'

'You are now, boy. Hang on to these. They're pullin' my pockets out of shape.'

He handed Mould four torches of the kind used by policemen. 'That makes eight. I'm trying' to make me some light. All day I've been trying to make me some light. I've got a problem, Mouldy.'

Mould moved into the evacuated area beside Red.

'I've got me a bobby-dazzler, Mouldy. I've got a mine to turn, but I can't turn it. But I've gotta turn it. And when I turn it I kill myself. It's wearin'.'

They came to a line of terrace houses three storeys high adorned by a parachute.

'In the attic?'

'In a lousy little cellar. You've gotta walk plumb over the top of it.'

They walked over it, out through the door, and down the steps. 'You're hemmed in, Red.'

'Mouldy, I'm nailed in.'

Mould couldn't see a thing in the cellar. Red said, 'When I joined the Navy I thought maybe I'd die. Well, I guess we all did. I thought maybe I'd die on the bridge of a ship in battle. I just never thought of dyin' in a cellar.'

'Don't let it get you down, Red.'

'Boy, I've been stewin' on this all day.' Red turned a torch beam on the tangle of timber and bedclothes. 'There's no way of turnin' this brute except one way. It weighs a ton, but I've gotta get my arms round it and turn it. And when I turn it I kill myself.'

'There must be another way, Red.'

'Boy, I can't go back and tell 'em I'm licked. There are thousands of people out there. Half a square mile of houses empty because of this here mine.'

They sat on the cold concrete floor and stared at the frightful thing in the beam of light for a long time.

'This is what I've been doin' all day, Mouldy.'

'Red, I'm not muscling in, but would you mind if I looked closer?

'Not me. I'm not turnin' away suggestions.'

'Don't block the doorway, will you?'

'I'm not doin' that either! I'm growing wings to scale those walls.'

Mould pushed his nose into the smell of it and his arms round the back of it, edging through splintered timbers. If the fuse started running he'd be hooked like a fish. He groped up, down, and across – and was pricked.

He stiffened and carefully withdrew his hands.

'What's wrong, Mouldy?'

'I don't know.'

He came to the light. On the tip of a finger was a bead of blood. 'Hurts like the devil. Like a needle . . .'

'Yes?'

'Red, there's nothing on a bomb-fuse that can cut a man. Red, I've cut myself! Red, it's a piece of *wire*! The aircraft safety pin is still in!'

'It couldn't be.'

'I'll bet you. I'll bet you any money you like. I'll bet you it tore on the bomb rack.'

Red felt for himself. He groaned into the mine that he embraced. 'A day's agony. That's what it's cost me. And it couldn't blow up if it tried . . .'

Syme laid out a third of a mile of barrage-balloon cable. At each telegraph post he passed it through a snatch-block pulley and finally in through the window of the parlour. Carefully, then, he turned it twice round the mine, shackled it to the aircraft lifting lug, and thought about it.

He was still thinking when he heard footsteps and he was out in a flurry to abuse the trespasser, but it was a brother officer, the one Englishman in the team of whom Syme was not certain.

'What *are* you doing, Syme?'

Hughie told him.

'You're mad. You'll blow the place up. You'll never move the car slowly enough.'

'If I shared your opinion, old boy, I'd not be doing it.'

'This I've got to see. But you *are* a newspaper man, aren't you, Syme?'

To the cable at the first post Syme tied his handkerchief to serve as a stretch-mark, to measure the elasticity of the cable. On that elasticity his plan depended.

'You'll never do it, Syme.'

'I think I will.'

'The first tug will fire the fuse – or the second tug will pull it over.'

The driver was waiting at the barricade. 'Thanks,' said Syme. 'Move her forward quietly to take up the slack.' This the driver did, then switched off. Syme now made a chalk-mark on the road in line with the rear axle, and another mark two feet ahead of it. That should be enough, he reasoned, to turn the mine.

'First gear,' he said. 'Smoothly. Ignition off. Ease her forward on the starter-motor. Understood?'

'Yes, sir.'

'Away you go.'

The car crept on battery power until the rear axle was in line with the second chalk-mark. The cable vibrated.

'That's it.'

Syme, his nerves in knots, waited for the explosion, but nothing happened.

'Thank you. That's where I want the car. Held there. I'm going back to take a look.'

His brother officer went with him down the quarter-mile straight, beside the quivering cable, round the corner and back to the post opposite the house. Syme's handkerchief had scarcely moved. Virtually all forward movement had been absorbed by the cable.

'Forget it, Syme. You'll kill yourself.'

The mine had not budged either, but the cable was rigid; mine and car straining at the cable like a tug-of-war between them.

'I'll try again.'

At the barrier Syme drew a third chalk-mark, two feet ahead of the second. There was a crowd watching. There was silence. 'Thanks, driver. Two more feet. Exactly as before.'

Two more feet on the battery while Syme waited for an explosion that didn't come. 'Lock the brakes!'

The Englishman smiled wryly. 'Good luck.'

'Driver,' said Syme, 'if it has turned I'll want you to ease the car off until the cable lies slack. Watch for my signal.'

He went back alone. Miles he had walked; back and forth; heart thudding, breath coming hard. The cable was *very* taut. How much longer before the floorboards split? Watching that cable; ready to run for his life if it fell slack. Round the corner again and the stretch-mark had scarcely moved! Absorbed by the cable again! And the mine hadn't budged.

Syme stared at the floor, at those shattered boards, and sighed, and plodded five hundred yards back to the barrier. It was a *long* way.

'No luck?' said the Englishman.

'No luck.'

Syme drew his fourth chalk-mark eighteen inches ahead of the rest. His features were set.

'Eighteen inches. Easy does it.'

Syme froze and the car moved.

He heard the snatch on the handbrake. He waited twenty seconds. The cable remained taut; the mine remained silent.

His brother officer was looking at him. What *did* his expression mean?

Under the barrier again, all those sad people watching, pacing it out again, never daring to take his eyes for an instant from the quivering cable. He refused to accept that his plan was unworkable. It had to work. There were reasons sentimental and practical.

There was the house that wore its parachute like a scarf. And there was the stretch-mark. *It had moved a foot.* And the mine had turned enough for his fingers to reach the fuse . . .

As the blitz continued the Australians worked on in Manchester, sleeping in the cells of the Salford police-station. Christmas dinner was a beef sandwich, a piece of cheese, and a glass of ale.

CHAPTER 7

Act of God – Wales

Cardiff was a peculiar experience.

'I've arranged for you to go down together,' Captain Currey said. 'Apart from Lieutenant Miller, it will be an all-Australian team. You're not wearing those big yellow L's now. I like the way you chaps handled Manchester.'

So they drove to Cardiff on 3rd January 1941 in good spirits, prepared to justify themselves. Accommodation was arranged, headquarters set up, and mines were detailed.

It was Red who walked into it first. He greeted the policeman cheerfully at the barrier. 'All clear, constable?'

'All clear, sir.'

Red's mine was in a railway-yard. 'Fix it up as soon as you can,' Miller had said. 'It's a fish-train on its way to London.'

Not far into his area Red came upon a group of men. 'Say,' he said. 'What are you doing here?'

'Minding our own business,' they said, 'which is more than you're doing.'

Red pushed back his cap and scratched his head.

Farther on through the lanes he saw others, even women. 'Say,' he said, 'scram out of here.'

They ignored him, and Red's anger rose. Then he came to his mine leaning like a loafer against the fish-train, but he had no intention of touching it while people were about.

He returned to the barrier and asked for the Superintendent of Police. 'Officer,' he said, 'I want all your men in my area at the main barricade.'

Red propped himself against a wall and waited. A dozen men eventually turned up.

'Okay,' said Red. 'Let's see you in a single rank.'

So he looked them up and down and said quietly, 'I've come a long way to delouse this mine. I can't be disturbed

58

by people. Will you get them out? Will you evacuate the place *properly?*'

He had to listen to a chorus of protestations. 'Okay,' said Red, 'that's what you say, but I say you haven't!'

They argued again until he snapped, 'Right turn!'

They looked at one another and at Red, and turned.

'In single file, quick march!'

Red marched beside them, away from the area, up the street, blood beating in his temples.

'Excuse me, sir.'

'Yes,' snapped Red.

'Where are we going?'

'To the police-station. You're under arrest.'

They turned on him in consternation. 'You can't do that.'

'Can't I? You watch! You bundle the last man, woman and child out of here, or else!'

Of course, of course. If he wanted *everyone* out. They had not understood.

That was the way it went in Cardiff. That was the beginning.

'Your first mine,' Miller said to Mould, 'is in a schoolyard. They drop them in some places, don't they? The building next door is the telephone exchange.'

Mould found it surrounded by sheets of ice and frozen snow, set up very nicely. What a mess if it had blown. What a mess there still could be. The fuse, to add interest, was a solid piece of ice.

'Before I start chipping, sailor,' Mould said to his rating, 'you'd better get out of the way.'

Given his solitude, Mould started with a screwdriver. It was a complete waste of time, and his big bang at Birmingham was still in his mind. There had to be an easier way. Not some crackpot idea like Hughie's salt, but something practicable. Like what? Maybe now was the time to start thinking. But something else started troubling him, for the moment inexplicable; then suddenly he was running for the schoolyard gate, revolver in hand. Something with an engine was coming, and no car, truck, or train was permitted within four hundred yards of an unexploded mine, for the vibration might set it off. Instructions to the police had been clear: *No vehicles through the barrier; none allowed.*

Mould rushed on to the road, wildly alarmed, into the path of an oncoming lorry, screaming at it, waving his revolver at it, but finding himself deliberately and provocatively ignored. So he shot out the left front tyre, so the driver crashed his vehicle into the kerb. Crashed and leapt into the muzzle of Mould's gun.

'You cut that engine, mate! You leap right back in there and cut that engine and get to hell out of here.'

It was a bad moment, and Mould watched him out of sight, all the way. Then silence came down again – and he was shaking. Never had he met hostility before and he was not quite sure what he would do if he met it again.

He turned – directly into a woman. His temper was so short that he cursed at her and ordered her out, but she caught hold of him weeping. It was like a dream of frustration. She was pleading with him and he couldn't understand her. Was there something about a dying father? 'I don't want him to die if the thing blows up.'

'Well get him out of here. Why tell me?'

And that was the heart of the story. She couldn't get him out. He couldn't be moved. So Mould went to the old man and said to him, 'First, please tell your daughter to go, to go out behind the barrier.'

'And you have to tell me,' the old man said, 'what this is all about.'

Mould did that – and the woman went. Then the old man said, 'If I'm too ill for an ambulance, what does it matter? You go ahead. I'll wait.'

Mould went back to his mine, strolled back, not at his best, back to the problem of his lump of ice. He considered it, and the idea that occurred was so obvious it was extraordinary no one had thought of it before. Hot water! Apply it, and the ice would melt! And there was a radiator *full* of it in his car.

Mould returned to the barrier, briskly and purposefully, filled a pannikin from the drain-plug, and hurried with it to the mine. This, he felt, was a simple but important discovery. He set himself up and allowed water to dribble over the face of the fuse. The effect was startling. Ice cracked loudly, and the fuse ran.

Mould's hair virtually stood on end. The nearest shelter was the school. He fled for it, imagining all the way the building buckling around him in the blast. Seeing the telephone exchange shattered from end to end. Seeing the old man killed in his bed. Seeing John Stuart Mould fragmented. He pounded round the corner and threw himself along the wall.

Twenty giddy seconds passed. Everything remained silent.

There was the hateful, ugly thing still lying beyond the ice-puddles, waiting for him. He was shaking wildly but had to go back to it, not daring to guess how many seconds were left. For how long had that fuse run? There was nothing to it but to continue as he had begun. He filled the pannikin from the car a second time and hurried to the mine. He dared not risk trickling the water again, so poured on a stream hoping to free the ice in a single piece. It cracked, and instantly the fuse ran.

Mould flew. He had five seconds; ten seconds; no more.

He flew for ten yards, then slipped on a sheet of ice. His heart almost failed from dismay and even as he hit the ice, even as air was punched from him, he saw his hat skating away, and expected to see nothing again ever. But the explosion didn't come. He lived a second, and another second, and fought again to run, but slipped again, and fell again, and gave up again. But still the end didn't come, and there was a terrifying hopeless urge to crawl like a frantic baby. He crawled and slithered and clawed off the ice and ran like a madman, blindly, until he was behind the building, flat on the ground, groaning.

After a while he looked again. The hateful, ugly thing was still there, beyond the ice-puddles. The lousy ice was still there too, and the fuse was locked up inside it, frozen again, perhaps, as soon as the ice had cracked. What margin was left now? Two seconds? Three seconds?

Mould found a telephone and rang Miller. 'This mine in the schoolyard,' he said. 'It's got me.'

'What's the trouble?'

Mould told him, and added, 'Where have I gone wrong?'

'You can't do the impossible, Mouldy. Burn the brute. If she blows up too soon that's bad luck. You've done your best. If you try again it'll blow up, anyway.'

'Burn it then?'

'Yes.'

Mould built his little platform and arranged his crucible of aluminium powder where molten metal could drop on the mine casing and burn through to the explosive. He lit his fuse of magnesium ribbon and retired to safety. Soon the grey streets were glowing with a fierce orange flame. Perhaps the mine would blow up in minutes and destroy everything in sight – but there was nothing more that Mould could do. Nothing more. Nothing except wait.

Five minutes passed. Ten minutes passed. And time dragged on.

At thirty-eight minutes the mine blew up.

Mould went back. The buildings still stood, all of them. Doors were blown off, glass still crashed to pavements, and in the schoolyard was the crater. But the buildings still stood.

Mould paid his respects to the old man, then went on to the next job.

Syme's position that afternoon was delicate. His particular weapon had come down in Prospect Road, Cardiff; a pleasant residential part of town; with well-cared-for gardens with brick walls and fine shrubs. Syme was a keen botanist and took the trouble and enjoyed the pleasure of exploring the gardens for the sound reason that he was worried about them. The mine had brought a wall down and was all but buried in rubble ten feet from a house. The house was undamaged and the district had suffered little. That made it touchy.

With great care Syme moved the rubble from the fuse, with great care and at great risk, and his finding was not a happy one. The external surface of the fuse was deeply scored, the neck over which he had to thread the gag was badly damaged, and the keeper-ring locking the fuse into the body of the mine appeared to be beyond moving.

'As a matter of interest,' Syme said quietly to his rating, 'I'll try the keeper-ring spanner.'

He tried it, but it would not engage. 'So that scotches it. It's a stinker, this one.'

Here was high ground falling to a crescent road which curved round the hillside. Had this mine detonated on impact, debris must have been pitched for hundreds of yards in all directions.

'A stinker, all right.'

The primer was damaged, just as the fuse was damaged.

'I can't touch the thing, sailor. Never in this world or the next.'

'What'll you do, sir?'

'Burn it. What else?'

'Close to the house, sir.'

'That's the luck of it. It'll have to punch a hole no matter what happens. Even the heat'll make it interesting.'

It was burn the mine or leave it, and he could not leave it.

'O.K., sailor. We'll set it up.'

They set it up, as far from the fuse as possible, lit the magnesium ribbon, and away it went in a flare of light.

They ran for several hundred yards and settled behind a high building, safe from any blast that could come from the spent mine.

'How long do you give it, sir?'

'It's been knocked about a lot. Probably damaged a lot. Forty minutes maybe.'

A brilliant flash of orange lit the low clouds and the earth shook to a horrifying sound. A blast-driven wave of dirt and smoke and stone cracked over the top. Half a brick hit Syme on the head.

It was extraordinary. The brick should have killed him, but he was too appalled to feel it. He couldn't believe the explosion had happened. It had to be a horrid mistake.

'Gawd, sir, it's gone off.'

The rolling dust-cloud reached as far as they could see. There were houses with slates off and windows shattered. The road was littered with earth and bricks and masonry. Muck fluttered down like snow.

Syme started running, sick with fright. It *couldn't* have been the mine; it *had* to be some other explosion independent of the mine. But on the hillside were the ruins. Homes and gardens had vanished from the earth. Roofs were stripped, chimneys were down, windows were gone. He stopped running at the edge of the crater in the midst of awful destruction, and swore helplessly, and went back to headquarters to report.

Lieutenant Miller was sorrowful. 'Chaps,' he said, 'Things have gone awry.'

They had suspected that.

'Look, Hughie,' Miller said, 'the Prospect mine. Are you *sure* you couldn't have rendered it safe?'

Syme was short-tempered. 'I couldn't get the gag on. I couldn't get a spanner on. I couldn't start.'

'I know you did your best, old chap, but I can't help thinking a more experienced officer, you know . . .'

'I *couldn't* get the fuse out. No one – I don't care how experienced – could have got it out. Lord, I never thought it would blow up. I couldn't believe it when it blew up.'

'But it did, Hughie.'

'I'm very, very sorry. It's the last thing on earth I wanted to happen, but it happened. Call it what you like – fate, act of God – I don't care what you call it.'

'That's the trouble, old chap. It's not God the people are blaming. There's Kessack arresting the police, Mould pulling a gun, you blowing up half a suburb. If Jerry blows them off the earth they take it. *That's* an act of God. But if the mine blows up when you're supposed to render it safe, it's your fault.'

'It's not my fault.'

'I know it isn't, but they think it is.'

They got together and fumed. They sympathised with each other, because they had never imagined that a community could resent their presence. The unpleasantness was caused not by them but by the ignorance of the people they had come to serve. Disasters and misunderstandings were caused by forces over which they had no control. They sympathised with each other, but something went wrong, and for the first time they snarled accusations at each other half-way into the night.

Perhaps they were ready for a rest. They nearly came to blows. Before they were through with Cardiff they hated the sight of the Welsh – and each other.

On the day of their departure Miller said, 'Mouldy, take a look at this map. This village. They've got a mine. No need to do it today. Run through to Gloucester and spend the night. Double back and fix it tomorrow.'

That was the way of it: routine. To Mould the journey to Gloucester and the run out next morning gave no warning. He had accepted Cardiff as unfortunate. It was obvious, despite their confidence, that this agonising business of rendering mines safe had affected them. It was obvious that they could not, ever, be unquestioned masters of their emotions, nor, *unless* they succeeded, could they rely on the sympathy of the people they tried to help.

Mould drove into the country considering those things, yet was caught again, unprepared. Afterwards, he tried to forget the name of the village, but the memory went with him to his grave. A fairy-tale morning, all the peace and stillness and charm of a vanished age. Snow hid the earth and lay over rooftops and hedgerows.

The mine was down a country lane. Mould, the architect, was enchanted. Usually Holloway, his rating at that time, went with him, but for some reason that he never bothered to fathom he walked alone.

He found the mine thirty yards beyond a break in a hedge, all but buried in a field. Beside it was a derelict stone stable; it might have been a barn; Mould never got round to taking much notice of it. It was odd how mines could turn up in such a place; jettisoned, perhaps, by a damaged aircraft or by a pilot off-course. He regarded it for a while, wondering what to do, but found the earth friable enough to scrape away. Everything was exceedingly cold, but it seemed that earth had prevented thick ice from forming over the mechanisms. He could work on them, and proceeded to clean the fuse and apply the gag. It screwed on easily and the safety pin popped home. The task now was to turn off the keeper-ring; these were rarely temperamental, but this one he couldn't budge. It was a fact: a man never knew from one mine to the next what problems were ahead.

He needed more leverage, a longer spanner. That meant four hundred yards back to the car. The sailor was waiting for him. 'We've got a long keeper-ring spanner, Holloway, I hope?'

'Yes, sir. Trouble?'

'No. Give me fifty yards and come along. When I've got the fuse out you can give a hand if you like.'

'Thank you, sir.'

Mould returned along the lane and came more or less abreast of the mine thirty yards to his right.

A cataclysm, at that moment, a flash that hurled him to the ground. The earth heaved into the sky and rained down by the ton.

Mould lay under the spread hedge, confounded, realising he had heard nothing – and horribly aware that he could have walked into the midst of it. Why alive? Why not dead? There was Holloway, crawling from the hedge lower down. They were alive, but the mantle of snow had vanished from earth and trees and cottages. Snow had gone. So had almost everything else. That lovely lane was as spent as a battlefield.

Holloway staggered to him. 'Are you all right, sir?'

'I should be dead.'

'Me, too.'

'You're not hurt, Holloway?'

'No, sir.'

'This is frightful.'

In the field was a horrifying crater. The broken-down barn was part of the crater, blasted into fragments, heaped high against the hedge.

'Did you hear it, Holloway?'

'Did I *hear* it, sir! My head's numb.'

'Look, man, we've got to find the bits. There must have been an infernal machine inside it.'

They searched through that crater until they were clawing in it. Then they became aware of an army officer standing at its rim.

'Yes?' said Mould.

'Are you responsible for this?'

Mould didn't care for the sound of that. 'It was my mine, if that's what you mean?'

'There's awful trouble in the village. You're supposed to have dealt with this thing. If I were you, I'd get out.'

So recently conditioned by Cardiff! So recently! 'Soldier,' Mould said, 'I'm no more responsible for this accident than you are.'

'I wouldn't waste time talking, friend. You get in your buggy and put your foot down. They're coming to mince you.'

So they ran.

CHAPTER 8
Kind of awkward – Primrose Hill

There was a welcome lull in February and March, but Spring brought the German blasting his way across Clydeside and Merseyside, across the Midlands and Essex, across Plymouth and Portsmouth. And London – where Syme lay awake considering a problem, while working parties cleared wreckage from the Admiralty. The problem at Primrose Hill!

An unexploded mine, of course, was no worse than itself. No matter where it landed – on a road, in a basement, or up a tree – its threat to the life of the officer was a fixed equation.

The homes of Primrose Hill backed against Regent's Park, but opposite, like a grassy hillside, reared the earth wall of a storage reservoir. That day Syme and his rating had taken an agonised look at the pale-green smudge of parachute rayon near the top. Set up beautifully for a glorious bang, for a tremendous thrust of overwhelming waters. A mine in the wall of a dam!

Farther along the same embankment a Captain Morgan commanded an anti-aircraft battery. 'No,' said Syme, 'don't you dare fire a shot.' Guns were out until the mine was out. That kind of vibration could trigger a catastrophe. 'What about my blitz?' cried Captain Morgan.

Syme had climbed the hill in dismay. The parachute cords were so short – so short they seemed to be. That dull feeling Syme had as he climbed. At the point of entry he found the vertical shaft the mine had carved. Smooth yellow clay down there, and the top of the mine, barely visible, *nine feet below*.

'Lord.'

They stared into the dark hole, Syme shaking his head. The fuse, eleven or twelve feet down.

They walked away a few yards.

'Do we dig a shaft, sir?'

'I don't like our chances. Every piece of clay we dislodge; every piece that falls . . .'

'And we wouldn't hear the fuse run, sir.'

'Would it matter? We'd not be getting far. The dam would be down like a thunderclap. Digging's out.'

'Which makes it kind of awkward, sir.'

Syme went back to the hole, heavily. The mine he had swivelled in Manchester had been a formidable challenge. Was this to be greater?

There was the road below, there were the homes of Primrose Hill, there was the Park beyond, all deserted, all abandoned. And here stood Syme with a ton of explosive beneath his feet and a reservoir at his back.

'My problem.'

He dared not dig, but was there another way? Could the mine come up to him? Could he erect a scaffolding, run a cable through a pulley, secure this end to the parachute shackle and the other end to a winch and *draw* it up? Like a tooth?

It was an idea. The winch could be set beyond the radius of vibration. The erection of the scaffolding would pose difficulties, but none insurmountable. What flaws were there? Suction. The tremendous risk of back pressure. That kind of pressure could fire a mine.

Well: could he sink a shaft *beside* the mine without disturbing the mine? Could he get to that depth without transmitting shocks to the bomb-fuse? One shock alone would blast the side out of the dam.

'Sailor, I'll come at it from below.'

Syme paced ten feet down the slope. 'From here, say, I'll sap back, down, at an angle . . . That's the idea. Let's look at it on paper.'

He lowered a line, and from its length calculated the depth of the fuse. But where was the fuse, *exactly*? He wanted to tunnel directly on to it, disturbing nothing, coming directly on that diabolical fuse to withdraw it and render it safe. After that he could go tunnelling for the detonator in reasonable safety. He supposed.

He had noted at other times that the tailpiece, that hollow shell which streamlined the parachute mountings, was lined up with the fuse always in the same way. A ridge in the tailpiece was always in line with the fuse. The ridge was there, plain to see, on the downhill side. The rest was elementary geometry.

'O.K., sailor. I'll do it. Scout around. Find me some digging-tools – strictly silent and strictly non-magnetic.'

That was Syme's problem for sleeping on while the Luftwaffe again rumbled overhead. He had started digging that afternoon, but a very short distance, and the battery on Primrose Hill was silent. That aspect perturbed Syme not at all, but drove Captain Morgan and his men to depths of frustration.

Early next morning Syme dressed for labouring, in dungarees and Wellington boots, although his digging-tools must have looked odd in the large hands of a naval officer six feet tall: a child's wooden bucket and spade!

The yellow clay was like new plasticine; soft enough to scoop out, firm enough to retain shape; and he drove down at an angle of thirty degrees, taking great care, keeping the walls of his narrow shaft smooth, almost sculpturing them. In an hour or two he was flat on the earth, working at the limit of his reach, still sculpturing the hole and laying aside the spoil, a small spadeful at a time. By afternoon he was *in* the hole, head down, wriggling in and wriggling out with one small bucketful each time. When light began to fade the hole was deep enough to swallow him. He waddled down to the road muddier than he had ever been before. Muddy and sore and seeping with the smell of the stuff.

That night the Luftwaffe was over again and the battery on Primrose Hill was silent. Syme made his way to his club to forget his cares and to ignore the perils of living. Mould was there, painting a word-picture of hazards so fearsome that Syme was convinced his own duties were on the privileged list. Mould took his orders these days from *Vernon*, not from RMS London any longer; he was a *Vernon expert* now, concerned with mines affected by water. Mould went ploughing through mud-flats and estuaries, and went deep-diving in harbours. He was off to Kent next morning. Red Kessack was already down that way with more mines than he could handle – particularly *watery* ones that he was not supposed to handle. Jerry, said Mould, had been banging in lots of mines along the coast and they were stuck in the mud, here, there and everywhere. Syme felt he knew about mud already.

During the evening a woman at the club guided Syme into a corner. 'I believe you have a mine at Primrose Hill,' she said.

'You do?' said Syme.

'Will you be able to render it safe?'

Syme looked at her. 'I'm sure I don't know what you're talking about.'

'Of course you do. The mine in the wall of the reservoir. I know it's you. I asked the policeman.'

Syme sighed.

'Now listen,' she said, 'that's my home across the road. My bathroom is at your disposal. The water will be hot. Everything will be ready for you.'

'If there is a mine where you say – if – the officer would be delighted to accept your hospitality, although he might be pardoned for asking how can the water be hot and everything be ready in an evacuated area?'

'That's my problem, isn't it?'

Syme was back in his tunnel at daylight, and he could move his arms and shoulders, he could twist his body and breathe. That was about it. He filled the bucket and wriggled out again, feet first.

That became the pattern for a while. It was easy enough

getting into the hole, easy enough filling the bucket, but getting out was an awful strain. It was difficult backing up all that distance, seven or eight feet, wriggling and squirming against the build-up of pressure in his head. Blood thudding in his head and pounding all over.

His rests became more frequent, and soon he had to compel himself to go on – against things known and unknown. The stink of the clay, covering him from head to foot; the depth of the hole, each inch bringing him closer to the mine and the increasing danger of shock transmitting to the fuse. Inch by inch closer to cave-in. Inch by inch closer to all kinds of things.

So he sat on the hillside, at last, and admitted that a limit was reached. Not defeat, but a limit.

For a long time he considered his problem. There were other ways, of course there were, but each one involved machines or outside assistance. Machines were too dangerous; outside assistance was not for mine-disposal officers. Again and again his mind came back to his tunnel, that dark tunnel, too deep and too steep. He knew he was only an instant short of lying in a grave of his own digging.

He returned to the car where his driver and rating idled in comfort. 'Sorry to break up the party. How much rope have we?'

'About three hundred yards, sir, in assorted bits.'

'Very well; let's have three hundred yards in one bit – *and* a volunteer, sailor, in a ditch three hundred yards from the mine. I'll have one end of the rope round my ankle, the volunteer will have the other. It'll be a hard pull every three or four minutes.'

'I've a strong arm, sir.'

'I was depending on it.'

So Syme went down his tunnel with the rope knotted to his right ankle, filled his little bucket, tugged sharply on the rope, and at three-minute intervals was dragged out on his chest.

By mid-afternoon Syme must have been very close to the mine, working with excruciating care, checking measurements and angles, and physically rotten with mud. The air below was foul, and even on the hillside smelled the same. Chest and elbows and knees and ankles were raw. Inside and outside he was raw, with pains in his lungs.

The battle against weariness was a cruel and overwhelming thing. So, too, was the battle against emotion. He was at the trembling point of endurance when his spade touched metal.

It was at once a victory and a fright. If this weapon were acoustic, actuated by sound, the next minute could be his last. He had come to the mine at 3.30 p.m. on the third day – and there he rested, head-down, for a 'while'.

Patiently he began to scrape the clay away through a time that seemed endless. Silence was life and sound could be death. He expected to find the bomb-fuse, but didn't.

No bomb-fuse.

Perhaps he had come in too high or too low. With painstaking care he dug deeper, and every few minutes was drawn up by the ankle and every few minutes wriggled down again.

No bomb-fuse, but *consternation*. The detonator coverplate!

Syme, in his yellow gloom, was confounded. The bombfuse was still locked up in clay far away, round the other side. For some inexplicable reason this mine differed from every other that had fallen on Britain. Either that, or the coaming had broken and twisted a hundred and eighty degrees. Of course it had broken and twisted, and Syme could have wept. The risks he had taken. The incredible risks – to be beaten by chance.

The rating met him at the roadside. 'What is it, sir?'

'A sad, sad story.' And Syme related it. 'So now I'm taking a bath.'

'A *bath*, sir?'

'That's what the lady said. So I shall be seeing about it.'

'I'll bring your uniform, sir.'

'An excellent suggestion.'

The door to the house opened to his touch. Over the deep carpet was laid a lane of newspapers, a white pathway into shadows. Syme took the path, trailing his mud, until he came to the bathroom. Everything was ready: even sherry and biscuits. He tried the tap, and the water ran hot.

The Luftwaffe came again that night and once more the battery on Primrose Hill was silent and once more Syme agonised on his problem. In the morning he drove in stately silence through the streets of London to Regent's Park. At the barricade the rating said, 'Well, sir?'

'Yes,' said Syme, 'You may bring your rope. I'll sap round it and come at it from the other side.'

'Round a curve, sir?'

'That's the general idea.'

'I can't pull you round a curve, sir. You'll stick.'

'I sincerely hope not to stick.'

He went back to the empty house to collect his working clothes. They had been too filthy to carry away and he shuddered at the prospect of getting back into them, but they were not as he had left them. Washed, dried and ironed – there they were. Somehow, during the night-raid, the woman had made her way through the barriers at the risk of her life. Syme had seen her only as the frivolous type.

The air in his tunnel had not sweetened, and down by the mine was darkness and dampness and the oppressive closeness of tunnel walls almost tailored to fit him. It was an awful place to be, to lie against the mine, inch by inch to encircle it with his body, inch by horrible inch underground. Fifty times, a hundred times up and down that cruel tunnel until he was all but stifled and all but blood-raw and by midday was attaining a curve in the darkness where he could lie listening and wet to steel himself for more silent wrigglings and squirmings. Never daring to touch the mine with force, fearing the inadvertent positioning of his body that would leave him jammed, trapped and dead.

Some time during the afternoon of the fourth day Syme

found the white metal fuse and removed the last trace of mud and grit before he began to render it safe. That he did, on his side, virtually imprisoned underground.

So Primrose Hill came back to life, and the patience of the ack-ack battery was rewarded by a night of jubilant action against the enemy. When the sun came up, Syme was at Bexley Heath with the fact of Primrose Hill behind him. From Bexley Heath he went on for several days from mine to mine until the price was suddenly exacted from him – a severe bronchial infection.

On Monday 28th April 1941, Syme was still confined to bed, and Mould, under the direction of *Vernon*, had deloused several mines along the River Hamble near Southampton. The blitz was continuing over the industrial centres and the ports, and in dozens of cities and towns the horrors of Manchester and Birmingham were re-enacted. Tens of thousands were dying. Scores of thousands lost their homes. Hundreds of thousands were in mourning.

Air-raid morale was a peculiar quality. In some places it was never shaken; in others it tottered, then suddenly irrationally, rallied when raids were at their worst or most widespread. Stubbornness, doggedness, or faith didn't grow out of pessimism but miraculously replaced it. So vital was this spirit that it became apparent to Germany that it would be impossible to defeat the British people 'by means other than extermination'.

On 28th April Captain Currey called Portsmouth and asked for Mould. It was an urgent call to the unhappiest duty Mould ever had to perform.

Red Kessack had been directed to a mine at Southport in Lancashire. The fuse had started running and Red had fled, but not far enough. Mould went up to Southport to take the remains to Glasgow for cremation. It seemed the right thing, to bury Red in the city from which his parents had sailed to the new world and where Red himself had worked with distinction during the blitz. Glasgow gave Red a state funeral from the great cathedral and Mould mustered an Australian cortège from a ship in port.

In less than a month the blitz, as a great offensive, was over. Red had died in its last hours. The German airfleets withdrew to prepare for the assault on Russia; 'Sea Lion', the proposed German invasion of Britain, was temporarily forgotten. The English Channel was a gulf Adolf Hitler could not bridge.

On 27th June 1941 King George VI conferred on Lieutenant James Henry Hyndman Kessack, RANVR, a posthumous award of the George Medal 'for gallantry and undaunted devotion to duty'.

CHAPTER 9
Man they couldn't kill – Lancashire

Germany, in those last hours of the blitz, set upon Liverpool and the Mersey. There were seven consecutive nights and huge losses and awful damage to the port and thousands of casualties and incredible numbers homeless. But it was a story not to be told by statistics.

Mould arrived during the afternoon following the first raid, well accustomed to horror, and resolving to close his eyes and concentrate on the job. That was to be his attitude or he would never sleep at all – so he said.

He booked in at the Officers' Club and was presented with a settee in the billiard room, but need not have worried about its extruding springs. He was out at night fighting fires, digging through rubble, comforting people, reacting as thousands reacted. It would seem that the odds against Germany were too great.

In the morning, dog-tired, Mould reported to Naval Headquarters in the Liver Buildings and was referred to Commander MS – officer in charge of minesweepers – and was taken to Salthouse Dock, where a parachute mine had been seen to fall. Its position had been fixed with reasonable certainty and Mould decided to drag for it, using the technique of wire rope, noose and marker-buoy. Commander MS remained present, having confessed interest in this technique. Mould hoped that *Vernon*'s glory would not be tarnished.

The wire rope was fed into the dock in a huge loop, both ends being held ashore. The loop, dragged slowly over the bottom, almost at once fouled the mine, the kind of evidence that impressed the audience and gratified the operator. Having located the mine, next step was to form the lasso by hitching a shackle to the rope, passing the long end through the shackle and attaching the marker-buoy to the running end of the loop. So simple that nothing could go wrong – unless he had hooked a heap of debris. The element of doubt added spice. The danger was the chance of disturbing the mine and detonating it.

Mould and two sailors began to haul on the long end. The buoy bobbed out into the dock, and the noose drew smaller and smaller. If they hauled long enough and hard enough the noose, in theory, should tighten on the mine until the shackle came in contact, *then* the marker-buoy should float directly above the mine. That was the theory. And that was the effect.

'Got it,' said Mould.

'Now what?' asked Commander MS.

'Row out, take up the slack in the buoy line, and lower a charge of amatol. We want the charge between five and ten feet from the mine – not too close – or we might have a big bang. All things equal, the charge should wreck the mechanism without blowing anything up. That's it, sir.'

'And that's easy?'

Mould shrugged and prepared his charge — or attempted to prepare it. Along the dockside rushed an elderly lieutenant abusing Mould with the fluency expected of native-born Australians. Translated, the abuse was a demand to stop messing about with mines while other poor so-and-so's were digging up bombs.

This was 'Digger' Fayne, a bomb-disposal officer who had drastically back-dated his age to enlist in the Navy. 'A bomb, Mouldy, a bomb! Three hundred yards from here. You set that mine off and the shock will set my bomb off. You trying to kill me?'

'Maybe you'd better show me,' said Mould, which was a request in character. Mine-disposal officers spent hours, days, walking round cities from mine to mine and bomb to bomb, comparing notes, weeping on each others' shoulders. 'Where have you got this thing, Digger?'

'In the railway tracks. Buried in them. Down between the sleepers. At the bottom of a dirty great hole.'

So they plodded off through railway-sidings where the smoke of fires still drifted and water from fire hoses lay in puddles.

'Over here,' said Digger, 'get yourself through these trucks.'

Over there about a hundred paces distant was a working party – five ratings and a petty officer. Fayne waved, the petty officer returned the wave, and the bomb exploded.

Mould flung himself flat as the earth threw up flame, smoke, debris and bodies cartwheeling in death. One came down over a ship and seemed to grab at the anchor cable.

After a while Mould returned to his problem. Fayne didn't have a problem any more. Perhaps Mould's would end the same way. One could never tell. Why had Fayne's bomb gone up? Three seconds later Mould would have been in the open, away from the railway-trucks, and dead in the blast.

He placed the countermining charge, paid out the wire to the firing box, took cover, and pressed the plunger. There was a tidy bang, the mine remained silent and unseen, and that was the end of the drill as 'laid down'. One could not present pieces as evidence, one could never say for certain the mechanism was destroyed, but that was it. The mine was supposedly countermined and its delicate mechanisms wrecked. This method would never do on land, but when a mine was affected by water different principles applied.

Mould declared the dock open to traffic and Commander MS said, 'We seem to have been more fortunate than Fayne.'

'We would need to be, sir.'

'We have another. Do you want a crack at it?'

'That's what I'm here for, sir.'

The second site was a small dock known as Canning Half-tide Basin, and again the mine was quickly located almost dead centre. Mould took the dinghy out to check the position and to lower the charge. Again it went smoothly. The same sense of dissatisfaction, but the same certainty that the job had to be done. He completed the drill to the letter, a drill devised by scientists, exhaustively tested, and pronounced effective.

Mould rowed out to recover his paraphernalia and allowed himself a thoughtful, uneasy pause of drifting, leaning on oars, with the mine in black depths below like a dead thing buried. He rowed back to the quayside, made fast his dingy, and mounted the steps to salute Commander MS. 'The mine is safe, sir. The dock can be opened for traffic.'

A shattering explosion blasted both men flat. An immense column of water and mud cracked over their heads and rained down by the ton. Canning Halftide Basin was sky-high, was falling in bits, and in the midst of mud lay Mould, profoundly sickened, stammering that he was appalled.

'Not your fault, Mould. You can't help it, old son.'

Of course he couldn't help it, but that didn't undo it.

'For G-God's sake, sir, c-close that Salthouse Dock.'

They closed it, a negative remedy, but no longer could a dock be declared safe when obviously it was not. They were playing with sudden and violent death, but didn't know *how*.

'There's no other method, sir. There's nothing else I can do.'

'Let's go back to the office. Let's clean ourselves up. Let's talk it over.'

In the Liver Buildings they talked it over. But no reason, known to Mould, could explain why a magnetic mine, under water, should detonate without a change in the magnetic field, and they were certainly not acoustic weapons or his dragging wire would have actuated them. The mines had been seen to fall, and in every outward way resembled every other magnetic mine ever seen to fall.

'All right, Mould, let's see the C.-in-C. Let's pour it out to him.'

Commander-in-Chief, Western Approaches, Admiral Sir Percy Noble, VC, supreme commander of naval operations in the west and the seas beyond, and John Stuart Mould, amateur yachtsman, civilian in uniform – face to face. Mould delivered into the den of the British lion.

He was welcomed as the expert from *Vernon* – with the utmost friendliness. 'Certainly, Mould,' said the admiral, 'if you wish to ring *Vernon*, use my phone.'

'Look, Mould,' said *Vernon* from the other end, 'we know the results of our own experiments and can only restate them. We *know* the method works. It has to be the result of your own countermining. You must have put your charge too close. There cannot be another explanation. So what are you to do about Salthouse Dock? Travel over the ground you know. The dock must be safe but if you must make doubly sure fire one more charge. Do that and open it for traffic.'

'Yes, sir.'

'But not now, Mould. Your call is fortuitous; we have been trying to call you. There's a mine at Barrow-in-Furness critically placed in a critical position. Tell Commander MS you'll be back tomorrow. You still have your car?'

'Yes, sir.'

'Don't lose faith in your methods, Mould. Accidents happen to the best of us.'

'I'm ringing from the Admiral's office, sir. I have him here. Would you like to speak to him?'

Had Commander *Vernon* heard? The reaction was a silence of genuine stature. Mould inhaled to repeat his question, but was cut short. 'It is not whether I wish to speak to the Admiral, Mould. Does the Admiral wish to speak to me?'

Barrow-in-Furness was a long drive north. Mould settled down with his troubles while his driver rushed him across Lancashire. Countermining had him deeply perturbed. Mentally it took him back to his first days in London when the future was to be greatly feared. The soothing words of his commander had not reassured him. He might have escaped more settled in mind had he not concluded the conversation with the most crashing *faux pas* of his naval career. He doubted if ever he would live that down. He wondered in fact, with more countermining ahead, whether he would live long at all. The Salthouse Dock problem had been solved by Commander MS by his volunteering to repeat the drill Mould had already performed twice in his presence. That one such operation had failed explosively appeared not to have discouraged the commander.

At dusk Mould's Humber came in towards Barrow-in-Furness at walking pace. Moving out were streams of people pushing their possessions or carrying bundles, camping in fields and under hedgerows, sleeping at the roadside with only searchlight beams and Heinkel wings to shelter them from the rain.

Mould found a boarding-house on the outskirts of town and rented two chairs. Germany was up top, but Mould knew he would live until he died, and his driver felt obliged to accept the same philosophy. It was a dreadful night.

In the morning, Mould, even wearier than the day before, heard that the mine was lying in mud in the Devonshire Low Level Dock. His Liverpool mines had also been submerged in the sludge of generations and he was still smelling the stuff twenty hours afterwards.

'I'll need a dinghy,' he said, 'and wires, ropes, shackles, floats, a buoy. And a couple of hefty sailors.'

'Whatever you say, Mould. Better still, give me a list and it will be ready for you.'

When he reached the dock everything was waiting, even the mine. It was a chance in a million, but bombs had wrecked a warehouse higher up, and a huge door had drifted down to meet the falling mine, to snare its parachute billowing behind. There were door, parachute and mine, midstream, and there they would remain until the soluble plug securing the parachute to the mine dissolved.

Here, as usual, were railway-tracks and a dockside built over mud-flats, and strings of empty trucks, perhaps twenty in line, and a tall building where the tracks ended.

'What's that?' Mould asked.

'A granary, sir.'

Here and there were workmen, many invisible. He could hear the ring of hammers; always the ring of hammers after the enemy had gone. He could hear voices from a submarine across the water. Hammers were ringing there, too.

'What's that?'

'A submarine they've sold to Turkey, sir.'

'This isn't going to do,' said Mould, 'it won't, you know. Too much going on. Hunt up the officer in charge. Tell him the sooner he gets everyone out, the sooner he'll be using his dock. If people start getting difficult refer 'em to me.'

Admittedly, Mould knew where the mine lay, but there were problems. The door had served its purpose and would now have to be cut adrift. The parachute, too, had to come off; cords and fabric would foul everything if he tried to lower his charge. There'd be one hell of a tangle.

Say, drift the dinghy downstream on to the door and let the ratings hold it there. Drop a couple of marker-buoys on the upstream side, untangle the parachute, and allow the door to float clear. Knot a rope to the parachute cords and drag the parachute ashore. The plug should break; it should be weak by now. Then carry on with normal drill.

His sailors came back and hammers had stopped and workmen were departing in numbers. Hurriedly!

'Let's get on with it.'

They rowed him out and tried to untangle the parachute. In theory easy enough, in practice it felt like a ton. They heaved and pulled while the sailors became more and more nervous and Mould's lack of sleep became more and more obvious. But eventually the door floated away and they knotted a rope through the parachute cords and paid it out as they returned thankfully alive to shore. There Mould mustered his team in line for a long haul to break the parachute free of the mine. Salvaging the parachute was a *must*. The cords were priceless. All over England bright-eyed girls with big-hearted friends were busy knitting sweaters – out of the yarn made from the cords unravelled.

'Right,' said Mould, 'it's a straight pull we're looking for.

Straight behind you and across the railway-tracks. You're not being asked to lift the mine off the bottom. All we're doing is breaking the plug.'

And so Mould, unknowingly, brought himself to the brink. German Intelligence had cracked the British system of countermining. The weapon in Devonshire Dock was not what it pretended to be. It was a time-bomb actuated by water, as Syme was to discover a year later. Clear water would fire the unit in twenty minutes; thick mud or sludge could delay detonation for hours or months until disturbed. The explosion could then occur at any second over the next twenty minutes, or mud might again send it to sleep.

They pulled yard by yard across the dockside, across the railway-tracks, and drew from the dock-bottom an immense explosion, an upsurge of foaming spray and a violent black shadow, a flying acre of filthy black mud. In his moment of horror Mould felt that the whole dock was going up, that the mass of filth boiling overhead would bury them alive, that the structure of his purpose and work was breaking over him to destroy him.

He found himself under the railway trucks with his ratings, found himself there in a storm of mud and an incredible predicament. The railway trucks, on level ground, were *moving* over the top of them, twenty goods trucks *moving* on level ground, with no visible force to shift them and no conceivable way of stopping them. Stumbling between the rails with hundreds of tons of metal rolling over them and Devonshire Dock crashing from the skies.

'Get out of here,' Mould roared. Into the open, into the black storm, with the dockside sinking like a plank underneath them, foundations gone, blasted away by the shock-wave; that massive dockside, that slab of weight beyond measure sinking into mud and spilling the trucks with it along the decline, drawing away faster and faster towards the great fat granary at the end of the rails. It crackled like an egg, that granary, and from the rent an avalanche of grain poured into the filth.

84

Mould was shattered beyond comprehension. All this in seconds. All this and more. Across the boiling water wallowed the Turkish submarine, listing forty-five degrees, wrecked. And underneath him the dockside went on sinking.

'Oh my God,' groaned Mould, crushed by his failure. 'All my own work, and so easy.'

The Humber hit the road again, back to Liverpool. There was nothing more for Mould in Barrow-in-Furness. The people left behind might be required to rebuild a dockside, salvage a submarine, and reconstruct a granary, but Mould had done as much as he was able. It was an odd world.

He dozed, with Commander MS and Salthouse Dock in his mind. So unsettling and insistent was the picture that sleep exhausted him. If the dock were open, he would close it again. He would accept *no one's* word, *no one's* assurance. Something was most dreadfully, dreadfully wrong.

He came into Liverpool late in the day and reported at once to Commander MS. He found Salthouse Dock was open.

'You must close it, sir.'

'I fired two charges, Mould, to make sure. Exactly as you detailed.'

'You must close it, sir. I'll not be able to rest for the worry of it.'

That was the instant of the deep throated boom of a major explosion and of a shock-wave through the floor they stood upon. An appalling coincidence; Mould and his eternal coincidences.

There was the explosion-plume, two hundred feet above the docks, tumbling into its heart of debris and depth.

They rushed from the room, driven by the same fear, rushed the car along the waterfront, and found new destruction and the bodies of seamen where Salthouse Dock used to be.

In a day or two Mould put Lancashire behind him, but he didn't forget it in a hurry.

He was never able to forget it.

CHAPTER 10
A week with George

On the way home, Mould paid a visit to RMS. That took him to London, to the Admiralty, and eventually to Captain Maitland-Dougal, Director of Naval Intelligence. Mould had to unload on someone. Maitland-Dougal was the benign father who watched over them all. He heard out Mould's story with a few nods and much silence. Silence was his trade-mark. One learnt by meditation.

After a long pause Maitland-Dougal spoke of other things, of a bomb-mine that had been given the name of George. Perhaps it was magnetic. Perhaps acoustic. It would fall like a ton of bricks, like an ordinary bomb; and was believed to resemble an ordinary bomb, even to tail-fins and impact fuse. There was a mine-unit in its after-casing, designed to explode in shallow water, but to lie dormant and deadly in deeper water until actuated by a passing ship. A very potent weapon with something extra and unknown inside.

Mould stayed round London for a couple of days, did a job in Essex, and made his way back to *Vernon*. He had prepared a lengthy report on Lancashire – not a record of achievement, but a list of questions. He had hoped to find himself talking things over with Hughie – Hughie, too, had shifted his headquarters from London to *Vernon* – but Syme was miles away mine-hunting in a river. A message was waiting for Mould to telephone his commander.

'Mouldy, have you heard about George?'

'Yes, sir.'

'Fenwick and Wadsley, lucky fellows, have got one in Glasgow. Really came down with a thump. And there's another at Pembroke Dock. That's yours, Mouldy. The Royal Engineers have demolished it, and I want you to get the bits.'

'I thought this thing was a killer, sir. How come they've got it in *bits?*'

'That's what you'll be telling us, Mouldy.'

Didn't have time to sit down. Picked up his bag and bolted for his car.

Pembroke Dock lay 250 miles north-west, near the farther-most tip of Wales, a base for Sunderland flying-boats in their war against the U-boats. So the Jerries had dropped George there and, as in Glasgow, had dropped a dud. Extraordinary, this business of duds. Unbeatable weapons that failed.

An officer of the Royal Engineers had taken George to bits. Had he known what he was doing? Probably not. He was the luckiest man alive, bar none. He had survived the booby-trap to end booby-traps.

Syme was always saying – what man has put together, man can take apart. Syme had heard another say it, but had taken it to his own heart. Mould was inclined to agree, up to a point. He was too close to Liverpool and Barrow-in-Furness to concur wholeheartedly.

Pembroke Dock was black when he got there, blacked-out and moonless and midnight. His driver delivered him to the office of the dockyard police. Yes, they knew all about it. They'd take him to the gentleman concerned. So Mould was the expert from *Vernon?* One of those chaps who lived with his life in one hand and death in the other? Mould pulled his hat down over his halo.

His Royal Engineer was deep in sleep. Poor man. Mould had to drag him out, but afterwards couldn't remember his name. All the mechanical components of George were stowed in a box. What Mould saw puzzled him. The entire mechanism seemed to be in one neat unit with two windows, diametrically opposite, inviting inspection. Each window was about the size of a spectacle lens, like a lighter-meter. What earthly purpose could a photo-electric cell serve in the middle of a mine?

'Jolly fine effort, soldier. Jolly fine effort.'

They turned the car at once back towards Portsmouth. Mould and his driver drove turn-about in two hour shifts. By noon they were home.

George was spread over the laboratory bench, and Mould as a quantity ceased to exist. Jolly nice of him to get it, but now his services were superfluous. In this field the scientists were the experts and he was a nuisance.

Those windows were selenium cells designed to develop a small electromotive force on exposure to light; sufficient to actuate a firing circuit. The instant the officer rendering the mine safe removed the dome from the tail to expose the unit within, light would detonate the full charge. Ah, the ingenuity of man. An impact-fuse for instant destruction, and two selenium cells as the final threat should the weapon be recovered. But in the first twenty-four hours the fuse failed the strike and the shock of impact destroyed the light-sensitive cells.

The scientists worked on into the heart of George – a magnetic mine, true enough, but different. The entire mechanism was housed in one compact compartment bolted to the tail. External access to detonator and primer, a feature of other German mines, was absent. The only way was through the tail – that fatal way. To reach the tail the *Vernon* expert was obliged to expose the selenium cells and destroy himself. Accepting that regrettable hazard, but untroubled by it on this occasion, they worked into the main mechanism. There the real mysteries began.

George was provided not with the conventional system of batteries, wires and condensers, but a sandwich of cardboard layers marked with peculiar patterns. The Germans had presented to the world the first printed circuits, a revolution in electronics. That was fine, but incidental on 15th May 1941. George was then a terrifying issue.

By this time the report from Lieutenants Fenwick and Wadsley in Glasgow had reached *Vernon*. In Glasgow, force of impact had so seriously damaged the mine that detonation was impossible, and the officers, observing the windows and imagining them to be inspection ports, had directed lights into the interior. They survived only because the mechanism was wrecked.

How were men to render this weapon safe, when it landed undamaged in mud or sand? How had Germany assembled it? You couldn't put the kick in after you bolted it together. The kick had to be built in!

The Germans assembled it in filtered light from which the lethal rays had been removed. The mine-disposal officer could not always carry filtered light, but he could work in the dark, and pray through his fingers. He couldn't switch off the sun, but he could wait until the sun set.

Mould sought out the bed that only his intense curiosity had denied to him hours before. He was tired enough to sleep for a week, but in hours they were shaking him awake. 'Sorry, old chap. There's an aircraft waiting. The Royal Engineers have found a George in Belfast.'

At the end of its whistling flight this third mine had struck a tree and somersaulted into the ground tail first. Incredible. Impact had ripped off the dome and ruined the mechanism. Mould took every precaution, but the Belfast George was dead long before he got to it: an evil-looking thing, pale blue, like an oversized, blunt-nosed bomb, of solid non-magnetic steel, with component parts far heavier than the corresponding parts of an ordinary magnetic mine.

Mould flew home through London. He took trophies to show RMS, an ill-considered move because Captain Currey had news for him. The fourth George was at the bottom of a hole in Stepney, complete, unbroken and undamaged. 'You're the authority,' Currey said. 'It's your job, old son.'

'Thanks,' said Mould, and headed for the club, determined to make the last night of his life a happy one.

On the morning of 18th May 1941 Mould drove out to Stepney. The Royal Engineers had excavated. At the bottom of a hole twenty feet deep was George, lying in a puddle, confined within walls of running gravel, a distinctly unpleasant sight. Would he have to sit on it to get at it?

This teeming quarter of London was deserted, except for Mould at the head of his shaft, alone, in the stillness. The hole was in a mews, with terrace houses rearing and old stables and garages crowding him. At five or six paces was an abandoned motor-car, which time, weather and children had reduced to dereliction. Perhaps he could throw a tarpaulin across the hole to darken its depths, but the sky was clear and soon the sun would bear on it. George would beat him by a mile.

Mould came back at sunset, some time ahead of Fenwick, his observer. Sam Fenwick's task would be to stand back, adequately sheltered, to record the steps as Mould began them and completed them. With a new weapon, *Vernon* had to know at what point of demolition the operator killed himself! The lessons learnt could be applied to the next George, or, at the worst, convince everyone that the task was impossible.

Mould had thought he had grown out of numbing apprehensions, but Liverpool and Barrow-in-Furness had shaken him. George was not the same problem, but Mould was the same man. On the credit side there was no known problem of noise with this weapon. If the observation post selected for Fenwick were close enough perhaps they could maintain contact by shouting – and thus avoid the hazard of telephones. Mould distrusted their wires and magnetised elements. Telephones were fine on the movie screen – in fictitious situations.

Again the silence was there, the unearthly stillness of an evacuated city. Mould all but trod on the cat before he saw her. She was mauling a pigeon, and he lost his temper and slapped her furiously. In these circumstances, at this time, she had no right to destroy. He gathered the pigeon into the warmth of his coat and found a moth-eaten rug to wrap about her on the front seat of the derelict car.

At the head of the shaft, five kittens started pestering him, full of fun and excitement. Wherever he put his feet there they were. He bundled them on the rear seat of the car and slammed the door.

Mould lowered his tools and went down to be with George. George who had hit the earth like a thunderbolt, but who for the first time had withstood the shock; withstood it so well that his impact-fuse had failed to operate! How complicated life was!

Here was George, undamaged, intact; and truly no one knew how it would react.

Mould scooped out the side of the shaft with his phosphor-bronze shovel until he believed he had room to lift off the dome; enough room and no more. He had no desire to weaken the shaft and bring the lot on his head. The whispering movement of gravel was not reassuring. So he went back up top to look for Fenwick, but at the first corner got into conversation with a sad cocker-spaniel sitting on the pavement crying to himself. He had come home to a deserted street, a silent house, and a locked door.

Mould sat beside him and explained the situation as well as he could and suggested that they should go together to the police station until the barricades were lifted and his family came home. The dog followed Mould and was delivered into the arms of a policeman.

There, waiting, were Fenwick and Hugh Syme.

The skies were black and streets were formless when they returned to the mine. Far distant was the rumble of the great city, but here were only shuffling footsteps and the murmur of their own voices held low by the very stillness through which they moved. Mould was on edge.

'Have you everything you need, Mouldy?'

'Yeh.'

'How does Sam get his information?'

'I'll yell – and you'd better stay with him.'

'I'd like to help.'

'It's my job, Hughie.'

They directed a torch-beam downwards. There sat George, in his puddle and spill of gravel.

'Long way down,' said Syme.

'Yeh. Join the Navy and see the world.'

'I'll give you some light on the rope.'

'Thanks. Then get back.'

Mould went down into the depths of his own shadow until George was hard against his legs. 'O.K. Back you go.'

Footsteps receded, then Mould was alone in blackness. He had not brought a torch. That would have been tempting fate. Knock the switch at the wrong moment and he'd never know the difference. That photo-electric cell was instantaneous.

Spanners. He had tried them for size earlier; one with short leverage, one with long. Ten nuts to shift from the studs that secured the dome. Only way to get at them was to straddle the mine, facing aft. He tried hard not to think beyond the mechanics of his actions, but he was a man and his mind would not be silenced. They had pulled George to pieces before, picked up the bits, sorted them, and mated part to part, *but with dead metal only.*

'I'm loosening the first nut.'

He turned the nut off and slipped it in his pocket.

'Second nut.'

His voice was startlingly loud, startlingly close, the distant reply so faint.

The second nut came away, the third, and the fourth, until he was doubled, groping, listening to falling gravel. All the way round the circumference until ten nuts were in his pocket and he was nerve-racked and incredibly tired.

'All nuts off. I'll try the dome.'

He had to shuffle along the mine to take the dome between his knees, and there he heaved and pushed and wrestled until he was desperate. He had neither room, strength nor leverage. And if it did come away, if it did slide back over the studs, would it strike the unit-compartment and fire the charge? The dreadful isolation of it. The anguish of it. No saliva in his mouth. No breath. No voice. A long pause.

'Hughie!'

'Yes, what is it?'

Mould looked up to the square of night sky. Hughie, so soon, so close? 'I can't shift the dome. It's too damned heavy – or I'm too weak.'

'You want help?'

'I hate to ask, Hughie.'

'Don't be an idiot.'

Syme came down.

'You're a sport, Hughie.'

'What's the problem?'

'Scared stiff I'm going to drop the dome in the wrong place. There's no room to move.'

'Less with me here.'

'You want to go?' Mould was breathing heavily. 'I've got to be relieved of weight while I get it off the studs and cover the windows. I *can't* leave those windows uncovered. You got a belt? Will your pants stay up if you take it off?'

'They've got two chances.'

'O.K. Join our belts. Loop them over your neck and round the dome. Can you carry the weight?'

'I can try . . . But it only needs some dope to switch on a searchlight, Mouldy . . .'

'You carry the weight. I'll stick the paper over the windows?'

'O.K., O.K. We'll try.'

Syme buckled the belts together and forced himself against the wall with shifting gravel under his feet, fragments pattering unceasingly, the dome hard against his shins. He hooked the loop over his neck and under the dome, and discovered he was bent almost double – with Mould stretching along the mine in acute discomfort: chests to metal, knees up, elbows back, heads almost in contact with each other.

93

'Strike me!' Mould panted, and yelled to Fenwick, 'We're trying the dome again.'

Syme heaved up to take the weight, incredibly difficult, and between them they forced the dome off, a fraction of an inch at a time, until suddenly Syme had it, bearing on his neck, all of it. Heavy enough to break him.

'Can you get your hands in, Mouldy?'

'Yes.'

'Be quick.'

Mould was still fumbling for the windows when the sirens started crying. It was uncanny. More, more coincidence! In the minute that the dome came off the sirens were crying. Selenium cells waiting nakedly for every searchlight and gun-flash and flare! And glued paper in Mould's hands that had to *stick*. Black paper that had to cover the cells totally. Pressed there, hard, by the flat of Mould's hand while Syme's back went on tearing and the belt cut deeper into his neck.

Gun-fire now, and aircraft engines, and searchlight beams in the sky. An incredible situation.

'This way, Hughie. Lean this way. I can take it.'

Mould got the dome away and lowered it into the puddle and an enemy flare burst up top, timed so precisely that it made a total melodrama of everything.

They sat there, the two men, side by side on George, with slush over their ankles, waiting for the raid to pass. A hundred things they could have said, but didn't speak a word. How close their lives had been to extinction. How close to extinction they still were, Mould with his hands over those windows.

The raid moved on and the all-clear came and Mould yelled to Fenwick, 'Dome off. Windows covered. I'm cutting the wires.' He dropped his voice. 'Do you want to go up, Hughie?'

'Hang that for a joke. Too dangerous up there.'

The switch was central, easy to locate by touch. Screws held the cover-plate in position; with screws and plate removed Mould could probe the interior and withdraw three leads. With these wires severed, the selenium cells would be harmless. The whole world could then, for all Mould cared, burst into light. Beyond that point were bomb-fuse, magnetic unit, detonator and primer – no easier or more difficult than any other mine.

'Three wires cut. Preparing to remove unit-compartment.'

Eight nuts this time, eight more to spin off before the compartment could be withdrawn. Only an unknown booby-trap could foul the works, and that was an ordinary, everyday risk. The unit was very heavy, but it came away and the sting was out of George's tail and in Mould's hands. It still could blast them to bits, but they would be unhappy wretches indeed if it happened now.

'Unit out. Removing primer.'

Syme steadied the unit against the body of the mine and Mould, by sense of touch, unthreaded the bolts that held the primer wedded to the detonator. It took time.

'Primer out.'

They allowed themselves a sigh.

'Thanks, Hughie.'

'A pleasure, old boy. What about the bomb-fuse? Tackling it now?'

'The bomb-fuse can go to perdition. Tomorrow will be soon enough for that.' They could hear each other breathing in the darkness, in the stillness. 'Hughie, I'm ready to drop ... Hughie, I'm going home to bed ...'

They looked in on the old car on their way out. The kittens were asleep, but the pigeon was dead.

At midnight on 23rd May, Syme sweated in a crater on the hill behind RAF Station, Pembroke Dock. His companion was the second living and undamaged George.

The night was compressed by heavy clouds, sticky, brooding and threatening. Syme's contact with the outside, sane world was a length of string laid across the hillside to another crater a distance off. There an observing officer, Geoffrey Turner, recorded each step of the stripping process as Syme tugged on the string – one tug, two tugs, three tugs – to indicate successive stages.

That night, at that time, Syme had death beside him for one fantastic minute. The dome was off the mine, the selenium cells were exposed to the unglittering heavens, and darkness was so close and intense that Syme's eyes were useless. He worked by sense of touch, groping his screwdriver from point to point until his hands had access to the electrical leads within the cavity. There could not have been a safer gloom, but fate was to time its attack with extraordinary precision, with impact far more startling than searchlight beams and gunflashes. Lightning struck between earth and sky. Light and sound simultaneously, so near, so violent, that Syme thought he was half-way to eternity. For an interminable minute of wild electrical disturbance he clung to that mine with his hands thrust over the windows, stunned with fright.

The storm went away and blackness was sudden and complete again.

Syme slowly came back to life.

CHAPTER 11

The great sands – Humber Estuary

Officer in command of *Vernon* was Hollebone, a young commander of considerable charm destined from birth to be known as 'Bones'. Mould and Syme were convinced he would have made a superb Australian. He had the right kind of humour.

'Syme,' Bones said one beautiful morning. 'Busy?'

'Always, sir.'

'A pity. I was hoping you could educate a Wren for me.'

'Never too busy to oblige, sir.'

'I have heard it said, Syme, that Australians know how to sail.'

'All Australians know how to sail, sir.'

'Splendid. The duty in mind, Syme, concerns the instruction of my Wrens in seamanship. We have two beautiful little craft doing nothing; referring, Syme, to the sailboats. A roster has been arranged; I would like you to alternate the assignment with Mould.'

Syme, despite pressure of business, found time to begin his new chore. The Wren was a sweet little girl, and Syme put on a show in the best yachting tradition. He explained the craft rope by rope and plank by plank and held her pretty little hand to the tiller. They sailed up the harbour and down again and a most excellent time was had by all.

Afterwards he told Mould all about it and they agreed that Bones was the salt of the earth.

Mould devoted the evening to a long discussion with Syme, concerning the intricacies of small craft. 'If the weather holds,' he said, 'I'm starting tomorrow.'

Mould waited at the pier in the early afternoon with a joyous sense of anticipation. Syme's animated account of the preceding day had brought a gleam to his eye that was matched only by the gleam in Syme's.

Down came a stern-faced woman with a fist hard enough to knock Mould into the middle of next week.

'How do you do?' said Mould rather sadly.

'Good afternoon, sir.'

'Are you ready to begin?'

'At once, sir, and I must say how much I have been looking forward to it.'

'Yes,' said Mould. 'Same here.'

He stepped down into the craft and offered his hand, but she made her own way without turning the boat upside-down or falling overboard. 'Jolly good,' said Mould and produced his inevitable grin and made a shaky getaway from the pier. When he had thoroughly briefed her (to the limits of his knowledge) he turned on the charm which no doubt the poor woman was expecting. 'Perhaps you would like to try the tiller? Don't worry if things go wrong. I'll straighten it up.'

She gave a smile and ran her eyes over the sails. As far as Mould was concerned they were in order, but when she asked him to tighten the jib-sheet he felt obliged to make her happy, and when she asked him to slack out the mainsail he thought she was laying it on a bit, but what else could a gentleman do? When she turned turtle he could always say, 'We must crawl before we walk, you know.'

But she laid it over and began to rip, as easy as darning a sock, and Mould congratulated himself on his remarkable talent as an instructor.

'You're a wonderful pupil.'

'Thank you, sir.'

She raced up the harbour and back again, down wind, cross wind, and into wind, and Mould began to raise his eyebrows.

'I say,' he said uneasily, 'have you sailed before?'

'Yes, sir.'

That explained it. 'With Commander Hollebone?'

'No, sir. With my father.'

'That's a bit odd, isn't it?'

'Odd, sir? No. I was his first mate. We've been round Cape Horn, sir, on a wind-jammer, twice.'

Mould swore to cut off Hollebone's head.

So they didn't teach sailing again! The Wrens were trained by Mould's pupil who held the Extra Master's Ticket in Sail. Probably there were not another dozen like her in the English-speaking world.

Syme and Mould did, however, instruct in other fields. During the autumn gales of 1941 small conical floats were washed ashore at Brighton. These were nuisance weapons laid by the enemy to disrupt the work of minesweepers. Whereas conical floats were not intended to sink ships, they were highly lethal on a beach, and *Vernon* was immediately notified. On this occasion Syme was met at Brighton by a Land Incidents party down from London. Life had become uneventful for the RMS men; the Luftwaffe had switched its attack to Russia; the only mines falling on land were due to navigational errors or combat emergencies. Despite the undoubted killing power of the conical floats they were not a major threat to the sea-lanes, and it was agreed that the Land Incidents men could profitably occupy themselves by delousing them. Syme was ordered to render safe these particular weapons and demonstrate the procedure.

Hughie cautiously made his way down to them through the defensive beach minefield, trailing his pupils behind him each man gingerly in the footsteps of the man ahead, then picked his float and squatted before it while the intrigued audience gathered round. It was like a dunce's cap, at first sight, with no apparent way into it. Syme therefore contemplated his problem and began to fiddle.

'What in hell,' asked one of his audience, 'are you doing?'

Syme shrugged. 'I don't know.'

'You're here to show us how to do it, aren't you?'

'That's right.'

'Well, how do you expect us to know what you're doing if you don't tell us?'

'I can't tell you,' said Syme, 'until I nut it out. I've never seen one before.'

The RMS party fled as one, up through the beach-mines, over the sea-wall, and far away.

Another RMS party visited *Vernon* to learn from Syme and Mould about mines when magnetically or acoustically alive. The two instructors differed little where magnetic mines were concerned, but differed profoundly on acoustics. Mould was of the opinion that the primer-spring should be whipped out in an instant; Syme believed it should be clicked out laboriously. On duty they endeavoured to present their respective opinions as alternatives, but off duty they argued passionately. Each was convinced the other was an idiot.

Mould met his first acoustic mine on Trinity Sands. Sands they were called, but rather they were fifty square miles of mud, past which at low water the River Humber flowed to the sea. Over this long and narrow mud-plain Mould and Syme often moved on foot, out towards the main stream several miles from shore, always with tremendous effort and often in great danger. Here they gambled against the irresistible force of the sea that more than once swept in across the flats with frightening tidal force and depth only yards behind them. Here each man knew that sooner or later he must face the dreaded acoustic mine in a most hazardous geographical situation. This was the vital waterway that gave access to Grimsby and Hull and was just too easily reached from German mine-laying bases.

Shortly after the course for the RMS that they conducted at *Vernon*, Mould was called to Spurn Point, the naval establishment at the mouth of the Humber. It was a long drive up into Yorkshire, and Geoffrey Turner went with him as observer. The officer in charge at Spurn Point had plotted the mine two miles offshore with cross-bearings on Spurn Light and the church spire at Skeffling. He gave Mould a wry smile. 'It'll be an acoustic unit; it's what they're sweeping, I'm afraid. Three tides have been over it, Mould, sixteen feet of water over it three times; and you know what that means.'

They knew all right. Alive, that's what it would be. And no active acoustic mine had ever been rendered safe.

It was at midday on 28th June 1941 that Mould and Turner and an apprehensive sailor manoeuvred along shore for the best starting point to venture out into the mud. A grey haze lay over the estuary, and the church steeple was not going to help much. Mould could not afford a mistake; getting bogged down out there was a sure way of dying, yet it was difficult to get anywhere without sinking knee-deep. And getting lost wouldn't even be funny. He *had* to find the mine; yet had to head for it without the benefit of bearings. Bearings were useless if you couldn't see the markers.

'Footwear,' said Mould. 'Boots are all right if you're feeling strong; they're mighty heavy objects to drag about. I'm going barefoot; I'd advise you to do the same.'

Turner accepted the advice, but the sailor said he wasn't putting his feet in that kind of muck for anybody.

They plodded out on a compass-heading through soft and sticky mud rarely more than ankle-deep. This gratified Mould and surprised him. Nothing like it had happened to him on Trinity Sands before.

In what position would he find the mine; primer or detonator uppermost? There would be no chance of digging around it or manipulating for more favourable angles. As he found it, that would be how he would have to take it. Scratch it or jar it for merely a second and the pendulum firing-points would touch. Jar it severely and perhaps the pendulum would swing the wrong way and countermine it, but only briefly. That same pendulum swinging back from the countermining position could easily swing a millimetre too far and complete the circuit and blast Mould's world to fragments.

If the primer and bomb-fuse were uppermost he would

apply the gag and attempt to remove the primer-spring by bull-rushing it as he had always planned to do; by removing the keeper-ring and in an instant wrenching the spring bodily from the mine. If the detonator were uppermost his future would be highly uncertain. He would then have to remove the cover-plate by unthreading four beastly, soft-headed screws – so soft they often burred or stripped – and then unscrew first the bung and then the detonator, both with bakelite threads that could grate, squeal, jam, or snap. Once sea-water had worked on bakelite, strange things happened.

Mould prayed for the primer; that was bad enough; but the detonator was almost certain death. How much easier it would be to blow the thing up from a distance, but the first man always tried.

That put Mould back in his environment, sinking in mud knee-deep, plunging on through filthy, sticky stuff, weighed down with the sheer wearying weight of spades and ropes and strops and floats and spanners as heavy as lead. The rating was in all kinds of trouble, fighting to stay on his feet, almost anchored by his thigh boots, almost trapped in them. All of them fighting on, trying to help each other, with mud over the knees, scared to go on but having to go on. For three hundred yards they drove through, exhausting their nerves and bodies, fearing the plunge into greater depths of mud, but at last realising that the hard bed was rising. It was a sense of relief beyond words.

They walked on, strictly to the course Mould had plotted, constantly alert for more soft patches, wondering whether they would have the nerve to push through another. Soon Turner was sure he could see the mine, a dark spot on the wastes where haze and mud merged.

'Half a mile, do you say, Mouldy?'

'Could be.'

They turned off and Mould's nerves were fluttering. Perhaps he was a veteran of thirty-one mines rendered safe, burnt, or exploded; perhaps all that; but . . .

They paced out a hundred and fifty yards – and the mine took wings and flew away.

A bird.

Back towards the unseen channel of the Humber, but now the mud was not without feature. Somehow it caught the light, and ahead it shimmered like a desert pool.

'We're in trouble. That's water.'

In a minute or two they stood beside a wide runnel – a barrier as effective as a high wall, which they regarded sourly along its vast sweep between shore and river.

'We'll not be going round it, Geoffrey; we'll be going through it.'

They waded out, holding their equipment high, and the water deepened until it cut at them icily about their waists. They shivered on through and pulled up on the opposite bank with chattering teeth while the unfortunate rating emptied gallons of water from his boots.

No sign of the church steeple, nor of Spurn Light.

'We're on our own,' said Mould. 'No bearings. And if the tide beats us back to this runnel we're going to look sick.' The rating appeared to be unusually dejected. 'And what's your trouble?'

'I can't swim, sir.'

'That'll shorten the agony for you! I think it's time to disperse. Say we search abreast, two hundred yards apart.'

They remained in sight of each other and went east over firm sand, an unexpected blessing. For half-a-mile they remained in station, then it was Mould who sighted the dark dot on his right and called his companions in, Turner from a quarter of a mile away. Mould waited on them in silence and anxiety, his life slipping away. That's how it was. No heroics, but disquiet, tension, and impatience. In an hour he would be dead. In the deep tank at *Vernon* Mould and Syme had demonstrated that bubbles alone, from a diving helmet, could detonate an acoustic mine, could set that acoustic unit prancing in a fever. Not a jack-hammer. Bubbles.

'You've got it?' Turner said.

'There she lies.'

There she lay. No doubt. Live acoustic mine, number one.

'We'll leave our stuff here. You stay with it, sailor. Coming, Geoffrey, to have a look?'

They walked in quietly and Mould was a curious mixture of racing fears and relief. He had guessed it from a long way off – the lifting lug was on top! That meant every vital working part was accessible: primer, bomb-fuse, detonator. Nothing was buried. Fate was giving him a chance.

'Mouldy, what a beauty!'

'Shut up.'

Turner flushed and Mould flared. This was a spell of silence not to be broken. Here in the stillness, beside the mine, all speech was irreverent. This immense thing on the hard sand; its drabness, its frightful silence, its huge internal ear listening to the whispers of creation.

Mould's sigh was soul-deep. 'Geoffrey.'

'Yes.'

'Shhh ... Record all markings. Numerals, distinctive features, and so on.'

Mould heard the pencil scratching. He could almost hear the mine listening.

'Geoffrey, leave the notebook with the rating for safe-keeping. And bring back the tools.'

'You're staying?'

'I want to think.'

He was alone with the mine, and for the first time since his days at *King Alfred* surrendered to sentiment. His thoughts were personal and homesick and bitter and desolate. He prayed to God. Until this hour his own courage and skill, though often greatly extended, had always been sufficient.

'Mouldy. Your tools.'

Geoffrey was back, squinting at him.

'Thanks.' But Mould felt three parts dead. 'Sorry to push you off again, Geoffrey, but would you mind telling the sailor to retire to a safe distance and lie down.'

'I have.'

Turner stood there, unmoving.

'Geoffrey, off you go.'

'I'm staying.'

Mould sighed. 'Don't be difficult. Be a pal.'

'That's what I'm trying to be.'

'That's ridiculous.'

'You've a job here no man has ever done. You'll have to concentrate. I'll help you concentrate.'

'Geoffrey, you are to go away.'

Turner shrugged and Mould took the tools and got down to it.

He applied the gag and regarded the primer in complete absorption for several minutes. This pause was a fearsome hardening of will, the prelude to transferring a drill from theory to reality. Rehearsed on a dummy unit often – on a live unit never.

Mould began, self-critical to the extent that he drilled his movements and disciplined every breath, but mind commanded body as he would command another person. He unthreaded the keeper-ring a fraction at a time, one seemingly endless revolution after revolution, each movement of less than a second's duration, each pause of at least three seconds' duration. It was the mind that toiled rather than the body. Time raced, but he knew nothing of it. Different processes. Different tools. Nerves and fear consciously forgotten, yet beating a degree above the dormant state. Nothing positive except the need to get the keeper-ring free with one hand and somehow hold the pressure against the retaining mechanism of the spring with the other. Difficult. The keeper-ring locked the primer-assembly and the spring into the mine. Deadly. Remove the ring and the internal mechanism was straining to leap at him, continually straining, trembling against his fingertips. If it slipped or writhed or twanged, the duration of life would be a moment. He sweated, unaware of streaming perspiration, an instant short of cataclysm. The ring was entirely free, and total pressure was pulsing through his fingertips to the hammering of his heart.

His fingers were inside the ring bearing down on the primer mechanism, but he had to take the ring away, had to move his fingers to allow it to come away, a delicate manipulation with death until the ring was in his left hand and placed aside.

Now he relaxed his hand to allow the mechanism to creep into sight and accessibility. He could sense the spring stretching, and he had to grasp it and hold it and control it in complete quiet, had to grasp it firmly enough to wrench it free, yet with not a sound or a fumble. There could not be a second of hesitation or a second of indecision. He was ready, but muscles and joints were craving for the rest he dared not give them.

This was the argument. Syme said he would kill himself. Syme said he would sweat blood for an hour only to kill himself. Syme said he could not pull the spring from the mine, true and straight, directly towards the human body. It was the body's point of minimum strength, minimum control and minimum reach.

Perhaps luck was to be a big part of it. Good luck or bad. He would never know. It would come at the count of three. Three seconds to crack the acoustic mine or three seconds to live.

Mould eased his body away, tensely, vibrating in every sinew, back to the safe limit of his reach, extending his rigid arm and bearing against the pressure of the spring.

One.

Two.

Three.

He wrenched the mechanism violently towards himself.

The whipping spring crashed like a breaking violin, and he crushed it despairingly to silence it, hugged it to his heart, sweating profusely, aching for breath. The mine lay motionless and silent.

Mould relaxed slowly and placed the spring down and

peered into the narrow tube from which it had come. Down there was the primer, against the business end of the detonator, danger still there, but not so delicately loaded. Silently, with perfect muscular control, he withdrew the primer and deloused it.

From the primer to the bomb-fuse. A brief check. The gag was still safe; so on to the detonator, the patient unthreading of screws, the tight drill, the short movement, the long pause.

After a breathless eternity his almost crippling control over body and nerves dwindled, and he stood erect, sighing, aching, looking up to the grey wastes. Mud, haze and sky were one and he was alone on the fringe of space looking into nowhere, but he had his trophies; spring, primer, and detonator; and he was alive. Mould saw then, in wonderment, the man beside him.

'Geoffrey, what are you doing here?'

'I've been here all the time.'

Mould couldn't grasp it ... 'What the hell have you been doing?'

'Handing you the tools. How do you think you got them?'

Mould ran his fingers across his brow, ashamed. How had he got the tools? He had no recollection.

'I put them into your hand as you needed them.'

What could Mould say? 'I'm very grateful.' Yet it sounded weak, so weak it had to be hurried over. 'Could you – could you tell the rating to bring up the strops and floats?'

'Of course. And what about the bomb-fuse?'

'It'll be out by the time you're back. The rest will be up to the local boys.'

Turner moved away, and Mould was alone with his triumph and his confusion. He was trembling with excitement and disposed of the bomb-fuse and its beastly mechanisms light-heartedly; even got his shoulder against that mighty mine and heaved it over by its tail to gain access to the clock. One ton dead weight, but he rolled it over. Wires were out and clock was out before Turner and the rating were back, and Mould's incredible achievement was complete.

The irresistible tide flooded in, and the three men began the race to shore, through runnels and terrifying mud, clawing their way back, exhausted and chilled and threatened by the sea to the last yard.

They returned to Spurn Point, bathed, and borrowed fresh clothing, and ventured forth. But the night was lost. They remembered its beginning, but lost track of its end.

There was another acoustic mine out there at that time, but not seen for another two weeks. When found, the senior officer at Spurn Point called *Vernon*, and Syme headed north. It was an innocent enough beginning.

Syme's reaction to Mould's achievement had been mixed. The patriotism of Australians was never entirely British. An Australian achievement was Australian property. Syme was proud, but puzzled. Mould had beaten an active acoustic mine; subsequent tests proved it. But Syme could not understand why. Tremendous luck must have gone along with Mould; and Mould acknowledged that. But, Mould said, an unsound method could not have succeeded.

Syme neither sought to detract from Mould's triumph, nor intended to do so; but his conviction remained unchanged. He would *never* snatch out the primer; but really his chances of meeting an acoustic mine were slight. The unit was undergoing continual development at the hands of the Germans, and they tried to put it where it would blow up ships, not where its secrets were likely to be discovered. There were rumours, too, of new mines that combined magnetic and acoustic features, mines that were to be cocked by magnetism and fired by sound, or vice versa – complicating the task for sweepers, and posing for *Vernon* a couple of wicked problems. Was a unit to be regarded as magnetically alive or acoustically alive or inactive? Would it, in fact, be identifiable at all?

'This mine, Syme,' said the senior officer at Spurn Point, 'is about two miles from shore. No boats, old man. It's a job for wading, and probably acoustic.'

Perhaps, thought Syme. But it had been there for weeks, and by now was probably dead. Without an active battery an acoustic mine was a heap of junk.

'We know it's been there for some time,' said the NOIC 'Dating from the last raid, it's been covered by sixteen feet of water twenty-six times. I suppose it could be said it's had every opportunity to go up.'

'Yes,' said Syme, 'I would say so.'

'Nevertheless, Mould had an active weapon, and I want you to conduct the acoustic test. I don't want a tragedy.'

Syme was an old hand as old hands went. Perhaps his anxiety for the acoustic mine did remain constant, but his fears were in the nature of a shadow without substance. The shadow was that opiate of man, that others may sicken and die, may be killed by bombs or passing cars, may blow themselves up, but nothing ever happened to oneself. And so it had been. He had resolved long back that no one would ever accuse him of carelessness, and no one had. Except for the explosion in Cardiff, every mine he had touched, no matter how dangerously placed, he had successfully dismantled. He had saved property worth millions, and lives beyond counting – and had reached the most dangerous moment of his career.

Two miles out, the mine, far beyond sight, a long and agonising squelch on a compass-course across acres of mud and sand, through shallows and runnels, an unceasing struggle towards the distant navigable channel as the tide receded. Tools and equipment were heavy, wearying, and irritating. It was a job for draught-horses, not for men. Out there, far into the Humber, Syme, his rating and an officer observer from Spurn Point came upon a C-type mine dropped by an erring pilot on Trinity Sands. Perhaps Germany lost the battle of the mines in her schools of air navigation. All the ingenuity of her scientists, the skill of engineers, the know-how of manufacturers, and the vast web of secrecy woven by intelligence organisations went for nothing because air navigators were not taught fundamental principles.

There lay the mine, slimy and muddy, on its side, bomb-fuse and primer uppermost. No sand; just deep, soft mud into which they sank calf-deep; mud that stank and stuck and held the mine captive.

That was the hard part. Slime and mud. Syme's instinctive reaction was to abhor its touch, yet he had to get down into it and wallow in it and somehow retain clean and sensitive finger-tips and a crisp, clear mind.

Was it acoustically alive? The serial numbers were buried. It could be a straight magnetic unit, and in Syme's opinion probably was. No matter what form its mechanism took, it was in all likelihood jammed by the penetration of mud. So Syme squelched round it convincing himself it was dead. There was no evidence to support his conviction beyond the fact of his conviction, yet he would treat it as an acoustic unit – gag the bomb-fuse, and remove the primer spring one cautious click at a time.

'O.K., sailor,' Syme whispered. 'Leave the tools and go back a quarter of a mile . . . And what about you?' he said to the observing officer. 'Watching the drill, or going with the rating?'

'You're *not* going to dismantle it, Syme?'

'Of course I am.'

'But the acoustic test?'

Syme scowled. 'Waste of time. It's as dead as the dodo.'

'It was an order, Syme.'

Yes, an order, and Syme had no patience with interference. Any form of interference was unwelcome. But the observing officer owed no loyalty to Syme. His loyalties were to the NOIC.

'All right . . . Acoustic test. Before you go, sailor, dig out the trace chain and the reel. Clank it, and I'll scalp you.'

The sailor departed laboriously into the haze, and Syme, with less than his usual good grace, laid out the chain behind the mine, and secured the line. 'Right,' he said, 'now we begin the work.' He heaved up the reel and held it across his chest. 'I'll draw on the line until it's taut, then you feed it out over my shoulder. I'm the horse, and the line's the cart.'

So it was.

'Right,' said Syme. 'Now are you staying – or what?'

'I guess I've got to. I gather you'd not be doing it if I'd remained at home.'

'You've said a mouthful.'

Syme trudged off, shin-deep in mud, and balance was his problem, balance without arm swing, while the line slowly unwound and passed over his shoulder. He had to support the weight of the reel and the weight of his bowed body and the sucking weight of mud. With each step he dragged up a bare foot like a cork from a deep bottle, and beside him the observer kept pace, step for step, squelch for squelch.

At about fifty yards Syme rested, panting, regarding his reel with disgust.

'What's up?'

'It's more than half-gone. Some hound has hacked a length of it and left me the short end.'

'And what's that going to mean?'

'Search me! Fifty yards, a hundred, two hundred – What's the difference? It's a waste of time, anyway.'

Syme heaved up a leg and squelched on, and the line ran out at about eighty yards. Eighty yards from the mine, and on the end of the line trailed the chain about to be dragged across the mine! If that mine was ever to go off the chain would put it off. *That* was the acoustic test!

'We're awfully close,' the observer said.

Syme took the weight with a shrug. He struggled on, knee-deep, dragging everything behind him.

They were enveloped in a vivid orange flash, were punched into the mud, cracked into it, against crippling pressures, kicked flat by a force at right-angles to their knees. Their legs almost snapped and their heads almost burst. There was a desperate urge to claw out of the quagmire that submerged them, that threatened to drown them in sludge, that choked up eyes and nostrils and mouths and ears and consumed all air and gave back none.

They clawed up to the light to be beaten back by a crushing sky that rained lumps as big as boulders; a murderous torrent of mud thundering with tremendous sound, burying them as they emerged, and burying them again; an endless mountain of mud to be climbed with all strength, natural and unnatural.

Then Syme discerned the quiet and the stillness and the stench and a body that ached to its last muscle. His legs creaked with pain. His head, throat, his very stomach seemed packed with mud. With every breath he chewed and spat the stuff.

Peace eased in over the quiet, and he was shaking violently, tightly sore about his heart, all but suffocating in mud, sitting in it waist-deep: the observer, too, a quivering lump of mud.

'That's that,' said Syme.

Beyond them lay six thousands steps to the shore.

He returned to *Vernon* the following afternoon, disgusted by his wrong assessment of the condition of the mine and by his offhanded treatment of it. He had marred his quest for perfection by carelessness and had meted out his own punishment. But the stinking mud that had almost killed him had also spared his life.

He reported the facts and climbed the stairs to his cabin to unpack. Somewhere, on the way, he was struck by a crippling pain, and awoke later in a strange room. He was hungry, bristly, but otherwise well. There was a window with a view. He threw off the bedclothes to admire it. Outside, a brilliant July morning, but inside most certainly the Haslar Hospital across the heads from *Vernon* on Portsmouth Harbour.

Syme rang for a nurse, waited several minutes, and rang a second time. Checked his watch and found that it had stopped! A forty-hour movement, but it had stopped! He rang a third time for attention, then lost patience and dressed and on the way out noticed a calendar.

It was not surprising his watch had stopped. It was three days since last he wound it!

He caught the ferry back to *Vernon* and remembered it was his week-end for a trip to Brighton. That was fine. On Monday he returned and wandered into the wardroom to prop himself up at the bar beside the surgeon.

The response was astonishing. 'My God! Hughie!'

'That's me.'

'You're drowned. You're dead. There's a search party. They're dragging for your body.'

Syme pinched himself. 'Not dead.'

'What have you done, Hughie? How did you get out of hospital?'

'Walked out. How else?'

The surgeon headed for the telephone.

So each had tangled with the acoustic mine. Mould had triumphed, but Syme had wounds. Mould may have rendered safe the only fully active acoustic mine ever rendered safe, but ahead of Syme lay Weston-super-Mare.

CHAPTER 12

The new order

With the passing of the blitz, rarely were Mould and Syme required to handle mines on land again.

German mine-laying aircraft still operated in small numbers against the approaches to ports, and E-boats roared at night into the Channel to mine the shipping routes. The pressure was off the British people, but not off *Vernon*. New types of mines were becoming harder to find; lying now on the sea-bed; and scientists could not rapidly defeat mechanisms they could not see. Yet Providence must have smiled over Britain. Despite the enormous efforts of men, *unaccountable* circumstances repeatedly gave *Vernon* the answers. There was Mould's strange adventure in the Suffolk village of Peasenhall.

Early in September 1941, a formation of mine-laying aircraft was plotted by radar off the Norfolk coast. From this formation one aircraft turned inland and dropped its weapon miles from the sea. This could not have been a navigational error, but a premeditated act involving the crew.

The mine fell in Peasenhall. A Land Incidents Officer took one look at it and called the Admiralty. In a few hours Mould was rushing to Peasenhall because this mine, fitted with two bomb-fuses, had been dropped with safety pins in. Pins deliberately left in. This discovery widened the conspiracy and implied understanding between the airmen and at least one armourer at the Luftwaffe base from which the aircraft operated.

Vernon treated the gift cautiously. They'd had gifts of that kind before, *packed* with booby-traps. It took Mould and a detachment of scientists three days to break the mine down to its components, but there were no traps, and it was an unprecedented free gift – the first acoustic-magnetic mine. The Sammy. So Sammy, like George, was beaten in a few days for reasons beyond the normal fortunes of war; a tremendous effort of German science and industry going virtually for nothing.

So it was that the old order changed and Mould and Syme went to sea. From there they hauled their trophies inland to a chalk-quarry known as Mirtle, and there X-rayed, probed, tested, and steamed out explosives, finally stripping their trophies, sometimes by hand, sometimes by remote control, through a growing barrier of booby-traps, and handed the pieces over to science.

The state of the German must have been consternation. Every twist of his genius was matched, and every new weapon was countered.

From mines that sank in comparatively shallow water he turned to magnetic and acoustic weapons that were buoyant, yet similar to the familiar cylindrical types that had been dropped from the air for two years. Code-named 'Tommy', these new mines were laid from fast motor-vessels.

As far back as July, Mould had recovered the first Tommy, adrift off Portland Bill. It was a hair-raising operation, but successful. He discovered a beautiful magnetic unit, different in design from earlier types, but subject to the same system of time-delay. Minesweepers were instructed how to deal with it, and then troubles began.

A complete six-day cycle of sweeping – the usual procedure – apparently failed to detonate Tommies even when known to be present. Perhaps a week or ten days later, disaster! A passing ship would blow up.

The German, it seemed, had introduced a new system of delay that threatened to destroy the campaign against it by forcing sweepers to operate daily for weeks on end in even the smallest areas. This was beyond the capacity of men and ships, physically and numerically. Yet why should it be? On known facts it was impossible.

It was accepted that a Tommy was a moored mine, generally encountered in deep water. If so, why were sweepers not cutting or snagging the mooring wire secured at one end to the sinker and at the other end to the mine. Where was the wire? In fact, where was the mine?

The answer had to be simple, and it had to be with the sinker. Undoubtedly the sinker could be adjusted to hold the mine at bottom for days or weeks before allowing it to float to the surface. This delay apparently operated independently of the time-clock in the mine.

'Right,' said *Vernon* to Mould and Syme, 'If you move heaven and earth, get us a Tommy sinker.'

Gale warnings were becoming frequent. Winter was close. Already buoyant moored mines were bowling up the beaches, driven from offshore fields by high winds and heavy seas. 'Yes,' said *Vernon* to Mould and Syme, 'all marooned mines on the coast of Sussex, Hampshire, and Dorset are yours, too!'

Syme was becoming hardened to the frustrations of each Tommy operation. He had chased them all round England, but every mine found had broken away from its sinker. They were searching not for a needle in a haystack, but for a grain of sand on the ocean-bed.

The call, when it came, originated from Portland.

A minesweeper had found a moored Tommy apparently vertical on the surface. Trouble had developed or it would never have taken up its unusual attitude. It was the first Tommy ever seen not freely drifting, the sort of sighting that should have sent *Vernon* into whoops of delight, but the commander of the flotilla ordered it to be sunk by rifle fire. He reported his sighting, but not before his marksmen had proved their aim and punctured it.

Admiralty raved and wept and rang *Vernon*, and *Vernon* raved and wept, and Syme found himself on the open road screaming west into Dorset.

By this time Mould had also searched for specimens of the sinker in East Anglian waters with *Vernon*'s floating laboratory, HMS *Esmeralda*. Mould and party, as a unit of the

Mine Recovery Flotilla, had groped at times perilously and at all times fruitlessly through the North Sea fogs. *Esmeralda* was now ordered to make for Portland with all haste to assist Syme.

Syme first joined the skipper of the offending mine-sweeper for an immediate search of the scene of the crime. It was out in the wide channel, with land dimly visible north and west. The sea itself was featureless, and the mine was on the bottom.

'It's down there,' said the skipper.

'Where?' said Syme.

The skipper reconstructed the known facts and produced on his chart a triangle enclosing ten square miles of sea!

Was it worth it? How could Syme *comb* ten square miles of invisible sea-bed?

The sweeper ran him back to port, where *Esmeralda* was waiting. A sight for sore eyes was *Esmeralda* – a seventy-ton private yacht before the war, but now a specialised vessel of an added thirty tons displacement. Strengthened and dressed to kill, the most heavily armed ship of her size, bar none, in the Royal Navy. Don Callieu, her skipper, loved her tenderly, fiercely and jealously. Not a speck of dust in all England dared settle on her.

Callieu and Syme discussed their problem. They had to accept that the search was blind, a foot-by-foot probe, and possibly the mine would find them first. Granted it had sunk, certainly the buoyancy chamber was punctured, but somewhere in the triangle was a mine still capable of destroying *Esmeralda*. Somewhere, too, was the sinker. They should have been connected, the evidence was that they were, but Syme came up with the staggering target of two hundred and eighty million square feet of seabed to be searched, virtually inch by inch.

Obviously, they needed a second ship, and asked for one. Whether they would get it remained to be seen. They wouldn't solve the problem by calling it hopeless, so devised a system of search using marker-buoys, lines, Asdic, and bronze grappling-hooks which, given time, would tear up every part of the sea-bed.

The next complication arrived with the ship sent to assist them. The lieutenant, RN in command of the drifter refused to stay with it. He had been instructed to deliver the ship to Syme, and that was that. He departed for the railway station, leaving Syme holding the baby in one hand, as it were, and an empty feeding-bottle in the other.

'What now?' Syme asked Callieu.

'Get another skipper.'

'I can't. I've tried.'

'Skipper it yourself then.'

'How can I? I haven't a ticket.'

'Now look, Hughie,' said Callieu. 'What the eye doesn't see, the heart doesn't grieve over. That's the Nelson touch. You have a crew.'

'Seven stokers, at least.'

'*Seven stokers?*'

'She needs them, they tell me, to hit four knots.'

'This,' said Callieu, 'I have to see. But the Admiralty, bless 'em, needn't know.'

'Needn't know what?'

'That she's your ship.'

'Don, it *won't* work. I can't even read a signal-lamp.'

'You have a crew: leave the handling to them and the rest to me. Make yourself invisible. Stick behind me as we leave port, beside me while we search and behind me when we come back again.'

Stern to stem then, or side by side, whichever the occasion demanded, back and forth across their ten square miles of sea, they searched in parallel lines and at the end of a week had found nothing, and the end of two weeks nothing, and the mists of November drifted in between the gales.

So much time, money and effort expended for nothing. Week three and week four. Syme passed the doubting stage and reached the worrying stage. Echo-sounders found nothing. Grappling-hooks found nothing. Was there, on the bed of the ocean, another ten square miles so barren?

From first light to dusk, seven days a week, Syme and Callieu steamed back and forth at dead slow. 'You must find it,' said *Vernon*.

In the fourth week, late in the day, *Esmeralda* detected an echo in waters she had covered before. Syme was not optimistic; also the weather was worrying him. The sea was up and the sky was angry. He had no desire to spend a rough night so far from land, and the old girl knew the way home anyway. He hailed Callieu and asked him to overtake.

Syme took her in, and seven stokers toiled to meet her incredible appetite for steam. He arrived off the harbour-entrance in total darkness and *Esmeralda* was nowhere in sight. Syme was sure he could get the ship through, provided there were no formalities, so took her in and was immediately challenged by flashing lights that he couldn't read. Signal lamps, Verey lights, amplified voices, sirens and bells assaulted him from all sides. A massive searchlight-beam burnt across from shore and fixed upon him. A high-speed harbour launch, 'bristling' with machine-guns, roared round him while its skipper screamed and shouted and suffered mild seizures.

There wasn't much that Syme could do about it – he couldn't get a word in edgeways – except continue wearily up harbour, which he managed despite everything and everyone, while round him the structure of British discipline and port procedure tottered between outrage and apoplexy. He reached his berth, went through the necessary motions, and called for his evening meal which, as usual, was corned-beef hash, a delicacy thrown together by one of the stokers. When, in a few minutes, a launch drew alongside, he was not surprised.

'Are you the captain of this ship?'

Syme admitted the sin.

'And your name is Lieutenant Syme?'

Syme agreed.

'You're to report immediately to the NOIC.'

That did knock him a little. He had expected the court martial to progress in easier stages.

'Don't keep him waiting, Syme. You've checked up a rare performance.'

Syme dropped his meal and was escorted to the naval officer-in-charge, searching his mind for defence, but finally realising that he had none. He had broken every rule in the book, and above all was captain of a ship without authority, sanction, or qualification. That alone could dismiss him from the service. More and more he regretted the paucity of his indoctrination at *King Alfred*.

With a mind almost blank he arrived in the commander's cabin with recollections of stern faces and of the gravity of his escort as 'Syme' was pronounced in the tone of a benediction. The escort withdrew, and Syme's world became one point of light, a shaded lamp over a wide desk. In its beam, illumined, sat a kindly white-haired gentleman.

'Ah, Syme,' he said, 'how nice of you to come. Have a cigar. I've been curious about your wonderful work. Do tell me what you're doing.'

On the afternoon of the twenty-eighth day Syme's grappling-line ran out taut, and before the line was in every man knew. The bronze hooks broke surface; and snared midway was the mooring cable of a mine.

Esmeralda edged in. That was the agreement. The danger of the triumph was to be shared. Carefully, over the next two hours, the ships manoeuvred the cable between them, and drew slowly from the sea-bed first the sinker and then the Tommy mine.

Syme deloused the mine on the decks of *Esmeralda*. The batteries, which should have been flat, were very much alive, and Syme had an anxious time. But Tommy was incidental. On the deck of the drifter lay a metallic cylinder no larger than a twenty-gallon drum. The threat of Tommy was beaten; the German had lost again.

Syme returned to *Vernon* with his priceless prize and an enthusiastic telegram of congratulation from the Admiralty in his pocket. He had scarcely eased into his favourite chair when they dragged him out of it. 'Next train to London, Hughie. Sorry, old boy, but don't miss it. Admiralty will meet you with a car. It's the Bristol Channel.'

Days earlier a flight of minelayers had raided the Bristol Channel and two aircraft had each dropped two mines unobserved. A few hours after the raid the tide had receded and an explosion came from a source estimated to be two miles seaward from Weston-super-Mare – presumably a mine detonated by its self-destruction fuse. That should have alerted the local authorities, but five days were to pass before at low water a puzzled observer glimpsed three dark spots out near the main channel. To Syme that meant, initially, a dangerous drive of four hours' duration from London in the east to the Bristol Channel in the west, where he emerged from his car exhausted by speed and nervous strain. But his troubles had not begun. He verified all known facts and the state of the tide, but they had called him a day late. The three mines offshore were without doubt Sammies with the standard magnetic-acoustic unit based on a six-day cycle. At the expiration of six days the clock would bring a destruction-fuse into the firing circuit by closing two platinum points. The mine would then be cocked, and nothing could stop its detonation when the receding tide reduced the pressure on the diaphragm.

This was the sixth day, and the mines had to explode at low water this night. They were far beyond reach, and tidal flow was such that at high water they were submerged to a depth of thirty feet.

'What can you do?' they asked.

'Nothing,' said Syme, 'and something's got to break. The blast from that lot will take every window on the waterfront. You'd better ask your householders to keep everything wide open between ten-thirty and eleven-thirty tonight.'

'Do you realise,' they said, 'What time of the year this is? You can't expect people to freeze.'

'I don't expect them to do anything,' said Syme. 'They're not my windows.'

Scores of windows tinkled to pavements at 11 p.m. The wiser ones endured the cold for an hour, and shut it out again at eleven-thirty, but only two mines exploded. The third lay washed by the sea, silent, and Syme already felt the certainty that the coming day was to be as dangerous as any he had lived. For reasons unknown, an acoustic-magnetic mine which should have destroyed itself had failed to fire.

The morning was gloomy and penetratingly cold, but by 10 a.m. a launch was cruising quietly offshore, two miles out, towing behind it a small dinghy in which sat Syme and his observer. The observer was jumpy. The unexploded mine was one of three, any one of three, and already the tide had fallen below safe depth. The diaphragm that had returned the unit to safe through the early-morning high water was no longer a factor. The mine was alive. Syme knew it and the observer knew it.

The launch purred against the tide, and drifted downstream ... and edged upstream ... and drifted downstream ... and back again ... and suddenly there it was. Not a hundred yards distant, a dark cylinder, startlingly close.

The skipper of the launch retreated into deeper water. Syme cast off. 'Move well out,' he called, then turned to his observer. 'Let's get at it.'

Syme rowed to within about thirty yards, taking his time, waiting on the tide. Why had the infernal thing not fired? There must have been 180 volts there, straining to go. Had the detonator failed? Had the primer, by a million-to-one chance, missed its mark? Had it twisted in the tube, stopping a fraction off centre? Had that superb example of the clockmaker's craft missed a beat? Was it running a day late?

The waters eased away in pools and lapping streams taking the launch far out, stirring up a strong and unpleasant smell like decomposing fish. Syme knew the mine to be a Sammy, no possible doubt, and it had come to rest at a bad angle – detonator uppermost. Primer and bomb-fuse were submerged in mud, an awful sight.

He lifted his long bare legs over the side, and the touch was breathtakingly cold and thoroughly repulsive. Knee-deep in water. But he dared not wear protective clothing. It impeded movement, and clumsiness was death.

'You can't work in that filth, Syme.'

'I've put up with worse.'

'If it runs you'll be stuck.'

'I've been stuck before, too. You just pray it doesn't run before you're out of range.'

Syme took his tool-bag and squelched to the mine, which was more in water than out of it. The stink was sickening and the cold almost crippling.

Still the water flowed away, unbelievably quickly.

The mine was cradled in mud. Six hours earlier it had been thirty feet beneath the surface. Now it was appearing above still receding water even while he moved round it trying to subdue the terrifying sucking sound his feet threw up. Only detonator and time-clock were accessible, but perhaps he could grope into the mud and gag the bomb-fuse. 'O.K. I'll be right. Off you go. Two hundred yards at least.'

What a place to be. Tool-bag in the sea because there was nowhere else to put it, and mud fastening on him like a gigantic mouth; the observer drawing farther and farther away.

He located the bomb-fuse and applied the gag with his sensitive ear pressed to the mine, straining for the first warning of vibration. But he could not have escaped, and might as well have spared himself the agony of listening.

He signalled the completion of step one. Step two was the beginning of a different proposition. Even Mould had had the primer to begin with. But for Syme, the detonator assembly! With his feet in water!

He began with his screwdriver, painfully following to the letter the acoustic drill, disciplining his body to withstand both smell and cold, but not succeeding. The smell was constant, but cold was cumulative, harder and harder to endure, harder and harder to maintain his sense of touch and steadiness.

The cover-plate came away, perhaps he was but a breath removed from collapse, but the procedure had not been difficult. Nothing had squealed. Nothing had stuck. Nothing had snapped.

On to step three; the black bakelite bung over the detonator. Down there, somewhere, the mechanism had failed. Somewhere between detonator and destruction-switch, along the main firing circuit, an unforeseen fault held one ton of high explosive an instant short of firing. Could he have come at an acoustic weapon from a worse angle? Not in a nightmare. He knew he would never hear the squeal of the swollen bung that would have to kill him, but he turned the spanner on and on, frozen physically frozen spiritually. Turned the bung on, and out, and into his pocket. Inside he was groaning. Outside he was silent.

He signalled completion of step three, paused a while, then inserted his numbed fingers into the narrow cavity to withdraw the two wires he had to cut to render this ghastly thing safe. The wires could not come.

Syme's stomach heaved.

He tried with extreme caution to draw the loop out, those few inches of slack that were the difference between living and dying, that would enable him to cut through with a strong clean action, away from the dangerous confines of the narrow cavity.

They would not come.

The wires were short — far shorter than ever before — and he was afraid to force or twist, afraid to wrench, almost afraid to breathe.

Syme hung over his mine, feeling the intensifying grip of the cold, and the tightening suction of filthy mud about his thighs. There had been moments before like this, moments of crippling danger, but never quite the same. Never with wires that would not come.

He signalled that he was in difficulties, and stooped there, alone, frozen to the marrow.

It was bad enough when wires were looped and free; even then, if the mine were alive, life and death were equal chances. If he cut the wrong wire first, he would earth the switch through his own body and blow the lot to hell. If his hands had been dry, if he had been standing on solid earth there might have been an escape; but he was wet to the skin and his hands were wet slabs of meat. He was a living conductor, with a hundred and eighty volts and a ton of explosive wired to his fingertips.

This was the penalty for touching the detonator before removing the primer. A calculated risk, that's what it had been, an occupational hazard circumstances forced upon him; but if he could have seen the wires, could have handled them, looped them, or insulated them by distance from the mine casing, he still would have taken his chance willingly enough.

Syme had reached a cross-roads, a point of danger past which duty did not compel him to go. Odds of death were too high to calculate. No matter which wire he took, to insert his pliers into the cavity invited the staggering risk of earthing the switch. What was the alternative? Destroy the mine by gunfire and break a few more windows along the waterfront. That – and destroy the reason for its failure.

Duty *did* compel Syme to go on. He reasoned himself into it. Rendering this weapon safe was *his* responsibility.

He tried to rub his hands dry, but couldn't. Everything remained wet; hands, pliers, even the detonator cavity. There was no way of reducing danger. No way.

He inserted his pliers, cruelly disciplining himself against his instinct to tremble, and at once met the next peril. His hand hid the wires from view! He had to grope, had to hope, had to pray that the wire he found was the safe wire, had to fight down raging fear and physical incapability.

He cut.

An explosive spit of sparks and a hundred and eighty

volts pitched him into the mud, spreadeagled him, clanged his pliers against the mine casing.

In his mind Syme died.

He had picked the high-tension lead – picked it red hot. A fully active mine, that's what he had, and what sort of miracle that this mud puddle was not a boiling crater? The nerve-shattering clang of pliers against metal should have put it off.

Had the acoustic unit failed? Impossible. The self-destruction switch and the acoustic unit each should have put it off. Neither had. The discharge should have put it off. Could he locate the same wire again and cut through it cleanly; could he do that and not kill himself? Except by electrocution perhaps?

The wire again, he found it, and a second time tried to cut. Again a hundred and eighty volts discharged through his hand and spat him into the mud.

He came up terrified, sore, and shocked.

A third time he felt into the fearsome cavity, and a third time cut with all his will and strength, taking the shock through clenched teeth, but severing the wire and numbly withdrawing his hand.

The mine lay silent, God knew why.

There was more. Bare ends of wire to insulate, and Syme had to grope for them without being able to see them, had to hang on with frozen fingertips and take sustained shock while he fumbled with wet insulating tape that didn't want to stick, but had to stick. That was his last hurdle, and it was a mile high. But Syme beat it and the rest of the routine.

A few days later his skin peeled off. From head to toe it peeled off, in strips.

Syme demanded of *Vernon* the clock from that mine; between its two platinum points was the speck of verdigris accepted in lieu of his life.

Conclusion

This story could have been much longer. You have read of a few operations taken from the records of two men. All told, they handled a hundred and forty mines.

Other men have crept in, but to none has full credit been given; a book could have been written around the experiences of any one of them. It has been a book about Mould and Syme because access to the material came my way.

It is, therefore, a story with a beginning and a middle, but not an end. The end is the beginning of another day. That was the pattern – never a total victory or a total escape – always the merciless call from duty to duty, whereas one such incident would have dispatched most of us to bed for a month.

Perhaps I could have given an account of Mould's brilliant work with those men of the P Parties, the human minesweepers. It was Mould who conceived the first safe diving-suit to operate independently of an outside air supply. Mould it was who devised the system of underwater search used by the P Parties during the Allied invasion of Europe, told by Bates and Grosvenor in *Open the Ports*. This enterprise, the human search for mines in the black waters of harbour-beds, docks, and canals, was considered so suicidal that official approval could not at first be obtained. However, so ingenious was the planning of Mould and his colleagues, all ports of German-controlled Western Europe were cleared without the loss of a diver: a miracle.

Lieutenant Syme, George Cross, George Medal and Bar, most highly decorated officer of the RANVR, was obliged to return home in 1943 to meet conditions of the constitution of the great company his family had founded. He endeavoured to return at once to England to resume his work with

Vernon, but permission was refused by the Royal Australian Navy. After a long period of futile and galling inactivity he requested his discharge in 1944 and returned to *The Age*.

Lieutenant Mould, George Cross, George Medal, ceased to be strictly operational soon after Syme's departure. He finished the war with Commander's rank, serving in Germany with the Occupational Forces for several years. At the completion of his term of duty he applied for repatriation to Australia, but was obliged to travel as an assisted immigrant. Under the terms of passage he was directed to employment with the Board of Works – a peculiar acknowledgement by Australian bureaucracy of his uniquely distinguished service. In time, Mould became Chief Architect to the New South Wales Housing Commission. Rushed to hospital with appendicitis in August 1957, he died on the operating table. Eight years later, in November 1965, Hugh Syme died in Melbourne after an illness.

The question remains: what enabled these heroes of such gigantic stature to function with sanity in recurring circumstances of appalling danger?

Their sustained heroism remains one of the proud mysteries and triumphs of the human spirit.